BIBA

EX LIBRIS

THIS BOOK BELONGS TO

_____

_____197__

BIBA

THE BIBA EXPERIENCE

ALWYN W TURNER

BASED ON THE PARI COLLECTION

ANTIQUE COLLECTORS' CLUB

CONTENTS

THE IN CROWD

DRESSING FINE, MAKING TIME, WE BREEZE UP AND DOWN THE STREET

DOBIE GRAY: 'THE IN CROWD' BILLY PAGE

It was like a jumble sale in the pleasure dome of Kubla Khan. The announcement in August 1975 that Biba, once described in *The Sunday Times* as the most beautiful store in the world, was due to shut up shop in little more than a month triggered a stock clearance that was as spectacular, as public and as chaotic as anything in the company's eleven-year history. The remnants of the clothes that had defined an era were piled in colour-coordinated heaps of finery, assailed on all sides by bargain hunters, style tourists and the morbidly curious, whilst memories and merchandise were strewn across the marble floors to be trodden underfoot.

It was billed as a closing-down sale, but the emphasis was more on closing than sales, and many who were there in the weeks leading up to that final Friday simply bypassed the tills, walking out with armfuls of designer clothes, bags of make-up, even furniture from the celebrated Rainbow Room. Shoplifting had always been part of the Biba experience, but now it was virtually sanctioned; many of the most loyal staff had already taken their leave, and there were few remaining who cared enough to challenge the hungry hordes of free-traders. And when the famous black-and-gold Biba carrier bags were found wanting, a supply of bin-liners was discovered to enable the goods to be shipped out more efficiently if not more profitably.

As the sounds of the Manhattan Transfer crooning 'I don't know why I love you but I do' drifted from the Art-Deco speakers, the true devotees of Biba were left shell-shocked by the devastation. 'In the armchair booths where you sit and listen to records,' it was reported, 'young men and women sat, oblivious of the chaos around them, in a sort of suspended animation.' Most committed Bibaphiles, however, those who had immersed themselves in the fabulous fantasy world that the store had offered, took one look at what they considered to be little more than grave-robbery and turned sadly away, determined not to pick at the bones of an old friend. Images of bereavement abounded as the committed sought to find words to express their sorrow: 'It's like someone dying,' commented one, 'and their clothes being auctioned off afterwards.'

The chief absentee amongst the revellers at the funeral feast was the founder and guiding spirit of Biba, Barbara Hulanicki, who had found herself forcibly divorced from her own creation months earlier by her board of directors and who could now only look helplessly on. 'Watching everything go was heartbreaking,' she said. For the faithful, it was

RIGHT: *Shoppers seek bargains in the closing-down sale at Big Biba, September 1975.*

her departure that had ensured the demise of the enterprise: if Biba had been a party – and it surely had been – she was its life and soul, and without her it stood no chance of survival.

She had opened the first Biba boutique in an obscure part of unfashionable Kensington just as London really started swinging in 1964. Three moves and nine years later, it had taken possession of all seven floors of the magnificent Derry & Toms building in Kensington High Street, enabling the company to celebrate its tenth birthday as the Superstore Boutique, the very epitome of style-conscious idealism and of that most sixties of oxymorons: non-conformist fashion. The seemingly irresistible rise of Hulanicki's retrophilia appeared to be a vindication of the classless aspirations of its time. In a world where actors, photographers and pop stars were the new aristocracy, Biba was their fashion store of choice, operating by quasi-royal appointment to Mick and Marianne, David and Angie, Terry and Julie.

That final incarnation, the two-year occupancy of Derry & Toms, when it became the first department store to open in London since the Second World War, is largely what has kept the Biba story alive. *The Sunday Times* said at the time that the only points of comparison were Harrods and Macy's, but even in that illustrious company, it stood out, an extraordinary creation dominated by the personality of just one woman. So pervasive an influence was Barbara Hulanicki that, even now, those who shopped in her store still talk of her on first-name terms; it was, after all, Barbara who stamped her image and her approval on every piece of merchandise. Walking into Biba has been compared to walking into a friend's bedroom, with their taste, their passions, their obsessions writ large for you to share: far beyond the limited range of dresses originally offered, you were now invited to participate in a style that embraced not merely clothes, but make-up, décor, furniture, food, pet-food, soap powder and more. It was, at its peak, a theme park devoted to elegantly wasted decadence and, if you shared Barbara's love of Art Nouveau,

BIBA FULFILLED THE ROCK & ROLL PROMISE TO LIVE FAST, DIE YOUNG AND LEAVE A BEAUTIFUL CORPSE.

Art Deco, Victoriana and Hollywood glamour, this was your spiritual home and evermore would be so.

For, uniquely amongst its brand-name generation, Biba has retained its purity and its mythic appeal. Unlike its contemporaries, the likes of Virgin and Habitat, it fulfilled the rock & roll promise to live fast, die young and leave a beautiful corpse. Born in Swinging London, its upward mobility followed a path diametrically opposed to that of the society around it. As the amphetamine rush of optimism wore off, and the country found itself heading inexorably towards the come-down of the three-day week, the need for a retreat into the past had become ever stronger. And then it crashed and burned.

'It really is the end of a dream,' noted Tony Benn in his diary in 1975, before glorying in 'the final

fling for the excrescences of sixties' fashion'. Others took less pleasure in the death of Biba, many now seeing it as the end of their own adolescence. 'It was such a huge part of us growing up,' mourns one enthusiast, 'and it had been taken away from us.' Another describes it as 'The end of an era on a scale with the day after the election in May 1979.'

It was the retail Altamont, the moment when it became clear that the hopes of the sixties were incapable of surviving in a corporate world of oil crises and faceless chain-stores. The Biba tribe, the beautiful people who had led the unexpected style revolution of the preceding decade, found their dream sold out by the stone-clad forces of big business. In the new age of insecurity, one thing was certain: the unacceptable face of capitalism wasn't wearing Biba eye shadow.

—————

'We were all lamb dressed as mutton in those days,' wrote Maureen Cleave of the pre-Biba era. Fashion in the Britain of the late forties and fifties was a dour business; aimed at the middle-aged middle-class, and firmly in the grip of the European couture houses, it was rationed out via institutional department stores that had all the allure of a municipal town hall.

The first sign that change was in the air came in 1955, the year that teddy boys carved up South London cinemas during screenings of *Blackboard Jungle*, the year that Bill Haley took rock & roll to number one in the charts, and the year that the BBC monopoly ended with the introduction of commercial television. A new, more populist Britain was being born, a reaction and a challenge to what was becoming disparagingly known as the Establishment, and down in the hip West End enclave of Chelsea, a small, related step was taken with the opening by Mary Quant and her husband, Alexander Plunket Greene, of their shop, Bazaar. Now seen as the first British boutique (though the word had not then been used in this context, making its first appearance in the press some two years later), Bazaar celebrated youth, fun and a vague bohemianism. It was still an up-market

*Barbara Hulanicki in
Kensington Church Street,
1966. The storage unit on
the left was inherited from
the previous tenants,
Home & Colonial grocers.*

distinctively alternative, and that drew inspiration from the emerging group identity of young Britain; Quant's clothes were purposely not the kind of things that a middle-aged woman could wear. And the shop itself represented a new model for retail: an independent outlet selling off-the-peg garments that were unavailable elsewhere.

The concept of the boutique spread slowly at first. In 1957 John Michael launched a menswear shop in King's Road, and two years later John Stephen opened the first of his shops in Carnaby Street, bringing what had previously been seen as gay style to a nascent mod market. Soon afterwards the Woollands department store in Knightsbridge introduced a boutique-within-a-store with its 21 shop, providing an outlet for designers such as Foale & Tuffin, Ossie Clark and Gerald McCann. Marit Allen, who edited the Young Ideas section in *Vogue* saw 1963–64 as the time when these small ripples began seriously to disturb the still waters of the couture hegemony: 'Things started to hot up, young people were finding a new voice; they didn't want to be like their parents.'

It was at this point that Barbara Hulanicki made her entrance.

experience, beyond the pockets of most Londoners, but the emphasis that Quant placed on the girl, rather than the woman, was a radical, even revolutionary, development that was to shape much of the coming decade.

Her designs drew on fields that were traditionally antithetical to female fashion. The uniforms of the schoolgirl and of the businessman were plundered and adapted to create an image that was

Born on 8 December 1936 in Warsaw, the young Barbara Hulanicki moved to Palestine (where she was baptised in Bethlehem) when her father, Witold, was appointed the Polish consul general to that country in 1938. Barbara was the first-born and two sisters followed, Beatrice and Biruta, both born in Palestine for, despite Witold's dismissal from his post by Wladyslaw Sikorski (leader of the Polish government in exile), the family remained in the Holy Land throughout the Second World War. In the aftermath of that conflict, as the campaign for a Jewish homeland entered a final, bloody phase, Witold found his diplomatic experience called upon by the United Nations in the role of mediator. It was a role that cost him his life: in 1948 he was abducted and murdered by Zionist terrorists. Within weeks, the surviving members of the family fled into exile in England, the country where Barbara's parents – though Polish – had originally met.

Here the Hulanickis came under the influence of Aunt Sophie (the older half-sister of Barbara's mother), an imposing, rich widow who dominated the family's life and, particularly, Barbara's later sense of style. Resident in the Metropole Hotel in Brighton, Sophie spoke English in an accent as thick as Marlene Dietrich's and enjoyed a ritualistically luxurious existence that involved at least three outfits on a normal day, more if she was entertaining. Her obsession with her wardrobe and jewellery, both unchanged from her 1930s heyday, and her attention to detail were to prove long-lasting in their influence. The rest of the family lived in a flat around the corner, decorated according to Aunt Sophie's tastes, which meant dark, sludgy tones – 'bright colours were vulgar' – with a marble bust of herself placed prominently next to the telephone.

In 1955, just as Bazaar was beginning to tweak the nose of British fashion, Barbara was 18 years old and leaving a convent school to go to Brighton Art School, whilst dreaming Hollywood fantasies populated by Esther Williams, Jean Simmons and Nelson Eddy. Best of all was Audrey Hepburn, whose appearance in *Sabrina Fair* she was later to cite as 'a huge influence on the Biba look … I was mesmerised by her shape: long neck, small head, apparently jointless and the first young person's hero to wear couture clothes.' It was Hepburn's image that Barbara drew upon when she entered a fashion competition run by the London *Evening Standard* that year; she won the beachwear section, the prize for which was having her design made up by the house of Norman Hartnell, the Queen's dressmaker. This initial encounter between the old and the future arbiters of style was clearly won by the Establishment: Barbara's halter-neck one-piece bathing costume was rendered in stiff taffeta rather than the polished cotton she had wanted.

Leaving college and finding a job with a Covent Garden agency called Helen Jardine Artists, Barbara became a fashion illustrator, drawing for the Fleet Street papers and for the likes of *Vogue*, *Tatler* and *Women's Wear Daily*. It gave her the chance to re-locate to London, which was welcome after the stifling environment created by Aunt Sophie, but ultimately the work was to prove too restrictive and isolating. 'I did about four years solid drawing; all by yourself in a room, you get awfully bored,' she later reflected. 'Another thing with drawing is you're so limited. You can't use colour. You're so limited that after about two years, you've done everything you can possibly do.'

Her restlessness increased following her marriage in 1961 to Stephen Fitz-Simon (universally known as Fitz), an advertising account manager at the London Press Exchange. First she left Helen Jardine

BELOW: 'Make the most of the little girl look,' urged the text accompanying Barbara's sketch of the first dress sold in Abingdon Road, 1964.

RIGHT: The first-ever Biba logo, designed by John McConnell.

to go freelance, and then, in 1963, the couple embarked on a new and potentially precarious venture. After years of drawing other people's creations, Barbara was encouraged by Fitz to design clothes of her own.

Lacking the capital to set up a conventional outlet of their own, Barbara and Fitz decided upon a mail-order operation, the one field where there were no overheads and where the money was received upfront before manufacture. The principle, they later explained, was 'High turnover at a low price'.

Adopting her youngest sister Biruta's nickname, the company was called Biba's Postal Boutique, and its first product was a simple evening skirt with a draw-string, advertised in the *Daily Express*. Two hundred pieces were sold, the garments being made up by students at the Royal College of Art in Kensington, under the direction of lecturer Joanne Brogden, who had taught Barbara at Brighton.

It was a quiet start, promising more than it initially delivered. For almost a year Biba's Postal Boutique attempted to place special offers in newspapers with a pitifully low strike rate – even when pieces did appear, they attracted little interest and few sales. It was not until May 1964 that the enterprise abruptly took off. A full-page in the *Daily Mirror*, commissioned by the fashion editor,

Felicity Green, promoted a pink gingham dress with a keyhole motif cut into the back and a matching handkerchief headscarf. The influence was immediately apparent: Brigitte Bardot had famously worn a pink gingham dress (designed by Jacques Esterel) for her 1959 wedding to Jacques Charrier, and had popularised the headscarf tied under the chin. 'If you feel that twenty-five bob isn't a fashion fortune – and it isn't...' promised the *Mirror*, then you too could buy into the look of the international jet-set. At the time the average wage for a woman in non-manual work was £12 12s: for under 10 per cent of a week's earnings, you could share the look of the most glamorous woman in Europe.

It was an offer that 17,000 women couldn't resist, and – with production handled by a Greek manufacturer, Theo Savva, in the East End – Biba's Postal Boutique found itself thrust into the heart of hip British design.

———————————

That gingham dress was in a sense the fruit of the seeds sown by Mary Quant. Bazaar had promised youth and fun, but it was catering for an elite; she described it in a revealing phrase as 'a sort of permanently running cocktail party'. Barbara Hulanicki, on the other hand, was offering sophistication that almost anyone could afford, and the response was overwhelming, with demand far exceeding expectation. In George Melly's words: 'Mary Quant appealed initially to upper-class women in Chelsea; what Biba did was open it up to shop girls. It was a democratic version of Mary

Quant.' In the war against couture, Biba was to provide the infantry: 'I didn't want to make clothes for kept women,' insisted Barbara. 'I wanted to make clothes for people in the street, and Fitz and I always tried to get prices down, down, down to the bare minimum.'

The problem for the average young woman was not simply price – clothes were definitely becoming relatively cheaper as more women found a place in the workforce and wages crept upwards – but the increased rate of turnover in fashion. For an office-worker, let alone a schoolgirl, there was a danger that the map of this brave new world of style-conscious teendom might be redrawn before it had properly been explored. If Bazaar wasn't the answer, and if the department stores were failing to meet the raised hopes of young Britain, then clearly a gap existed in the market – and Biba's Postal Boutique was ready to take up the challenge.

Further offers followed in the *Mirror* and in *Honey* magazine (launched in 1960 and fast becoming the consumer Bible for girls), before Barbara decided that the time had come to try opening a shop, 'just as a hobby'. Despite the initial misgivings of Fitz, an overdraft of £2,000 was secured, premises were acquired at a rent of £20 a week, and the first Biba shop was opened on 7 September 1964.

The location was unimpressive. Abingdon Road in Kensington, West London wasn't that far from Bazaar and John Michael in Chelsea, but it was far enough to make all the difference, while the real centre of fashionable London was in Mayfair and Soho, which seemed like another world entirely.

Kensington at that time was neither gear nor groovy; it was sedate, elderly and genteel, its principal shopping area dominated by three archetypal department stores of the old school: Barker's, Derry & Toms and Pontings. It was a place for old ladies and afternoon tea. And the premises themselves at number 87 weren't exactly prepossessing. It was a Victorian corner shop that had once – some time ago – been a chemist. The external paint was peeling, the interior needed redecorating and the floor-space was tiny.

Nonetheless, it was cheap and, Barbara believed, it had potential, particularly once a new floor of black and white tiles had been laid, and Fitz had painted the walls a dark navy. Thereafter the money ran out and, turning necessity into a virtue, it was decided to leave the shabby exterior as it was. Similarly the funds were not available for normal display rails, and an alternative was found in the Victorian bentwood hat stands that were then so deeply unfashionable that they could be picked up for a song at street markets. Clothes were to be hung from these free-standing units in the middle of the floor while a table served as a cash desk. No sign was painted above the shop, but the style of the existing windows, painted halfway up in black and gold, was retained. John McConnell, a young designer whose wife, Moira MacGregor, had worked with Barbara at Helen Jardine Artists, had already created a logo for Biba's Postal Boutique: a circle with the company name in it echoed the image of a cancelling stamp. Now he painted the windows in a style that paid homage to the company's origins: an envelope design picked out in gold on

black with the Biba stamp. It was, he remembers, a low-budget affair: 'Very crude, very basic, something like black emulsion and tape.' (The logo itself did not appear at this stage on the clothes themselves, which had no identifying brand at all, thus cutting costs further.)

With the windows half blacked out, and with very subdued lighting inside, it was a dark, conspiratorial

IT WAS A SORT OF ALI BABA, CASBAH KIND OF THING

and crowded environment, full of mystery and promise. Barbara was later to say that her idea was that she 'thought French boutiques looked like that', but the general impression was of something simultaneously exotic and welcoming. It was a 'sort of Ali Baba, Casbah kind of thing', said Julie Hodgess, who later designed the wallpaper for the store, while McConnell remembers it as 'a boudoir, a girl's place of secret passion and secret events'. For those who frequented the shop, it was even more personal than that: 'It was a bit like going into someone's house,' remembers one, whilst the presence of Barbara and Fitz in the shop, mingling with the customers, gave the tone of a family-run restaurant.

The roles of the personnel were already fixed at this early stage. Barbara was responsible for the design and creative elements, whilst Fitz handled all the business affairs: 'He doesn't want to know my side of it, I don't want to know his, so it works out terribly well.' Also firmly established was the

practice that would survive the entire life of Biba, that the shop assistants were never to approach the customers; Barbara always insisted that she 'couldn't stand those old bags who ram clothes down your throat', and she was adamant from the outset that no employee of hers would ever utter the dread words, 'Can I help you, madam?' Thus the stories of the aloof, disdainful Biba girls began. The one exception, remembers Simon Jenkins, later the editor of *The Times* and then a neighbour, was when men turned up with their girlfriends – since it was assumed that it was the man who would end up paying for the clothes, he was made to feel welcome and treated extremely well.

What Biba was helping to create was the concept of shopping as an experience, a leisure activity for the young. Breaking from the fifties pattern, this was no longer something that a girl did reluctantly with her mother, it was a social event in its own right to be shared with peers. Those who knew about Biba – and despite the lack of a name above the shop, despite the obscure location, there were plenty who did – saw it as being an essential place to meet and be seen.

The absence of advertising didn't mean that Biba lacked a public face. Crucial to the success of the shop was the endorsement of Cathy McGowan on the TV pop show *Ready Steady Go!* Originally employed by the programme as a kind of sounding-board consultant, having responded to an advert asking for a 'typical teenager', McGowan had been thrust into the role of presenter and had rapidly become one of the most recognisable figures in youth culture. And when she was introduced to

Biba – via a double-page spread in *Honey* – she also became the most visible wearer of Barbara's designs. Broadcast by Associated Rediffusion on Friday nights, *Ready Steady Go!* seldom achieved massive viewing figures (four to five million was its normal mark), but for a brief period between 1963 and 1966, as the Beatles and the Stones shared a stage with the stars of Motown and Stax, it was the hippest programme on Earth, reaching precisely the market that would respond to Biba's cool appeal. And in a world of dolly birds, it had in McGowan the *uber*-dolly, a girl whose very ordinariness made her an achievable role model. The show's slogan of 'The weekend starts here' was no more than the truth for Biba: '*Ready Steady Go!* was the showcase: dress Cathy McGowan on Friday, and on Saturday there were queues round the block.'

The clothes that were sold in that first shop were simple and limited. Following Bazaar's lead, the emphasis was on youthful styles. Indeed Barbara took the approach further, back almost to childhood: 'Mary Quant's clothes were slightly older, more serious, adult in a way,' remembers one shopper, whereas 'Biba was very young, very trendy.' For others, the pieces had echoes of pre-sexuality: 'They were very little-girly shapes, no cleavage, it was rather androgynous.' Barbara was happy to take a material like knitted cotton jersey, previously associated with children's underwear, and use it for a dress, or to adapt a traditional rugby shirt to become a mini-dress, suitably dyed in what were becoming Biba's trademark dark colours.

On the very first day there was just one garment available – a brown smock in a chalk pinstripe –

and even that was offered in only one size. Nonetheless, it sold out immediately, setting a pattern for the next couple of years. Eschewing such traditional concepts as seasons, Biba specialised in short runs. 'The youngsters loved our stuff because it was not mass produced,' Barbara later explained. 'It wasn't seasonal; it just rolled over all the time.' Which meant, of course, that you had to be quick off the mark, as Twiggy remembered: 'If you didn't buy what you wanted there and then, it wasn't worth coming back next week and hoping it would still be there.' Another retailer for whom he was working asked John McConnell what Biba's stock turnover was: 'He said, "How many times a year does the stock sell out?" And I said, "Oh, twice a day." Because by midday the shop was empty, and there was another lorry-load coming up from the East End to fill it.'

It may have been a slight exaggeration, but it was at least the case on the weekend. With so many of its customers working during the week, or even still at school, Biba on Saturday became the highpoint of the week, 'A place of pilgrimage for office girls seeking refuge from the dull dreary department store offerings,' as the *Evening Standard* put it. It was the day that the new stock was delivered and the day that the shop was overrun with customers. Extra staff were employed on the weekend to cope with the rush, amongst them Sarah Burnett, enticed not so much by the wages as by the fringe benefits: 'There was this amazing delivery on a Saturday morning, and so all the people who worked there got the pick of the new stuff. I believe that's why I worked there.'

That sense of wanting to be the first with the new styles, of belonging to a world where everything was immediate and now, was crucial to the popularity of the boutique. These clothes weren't built to last, they were for the moment, and by embracing the rapid turnover and introduction of new lines, one was declaring oneself in tune with the mood of new Britain, as Terence Conran – whose Habitat store opened the same year as Biba – was quick to observe: 'People have become enormously aware of colour and design, and they are prepared to have more exciting things provided they are less expensive and more expendable.'

The phrase had yet to be coined, but here the personal was political; this was a revolution, albeit an intimate, personal revolution, as George Melly points out: 'It didn't intimidate, but it did produce things that mothers would dislike.' Barbara herself saw it better than anyone: 'The mothers of the girls who hung out at Biba used to attack us because it was such a dark place and the clothes were dark and the music was loud. But the more they yelled the better it was. Young people flock to dark places and at the beginning the less they could see what they were buying, the louder the music, the more scrambled their brains, the happier they were.'

———

On 16 April 1965 the *Daily Telegraph* published an article by John Crosby headlined 'London: the most exciting city in the world', the piece that first articulated the concept of Swinging London. Illustrating the celebration of a social life that was 'vibrating with youth', and which congregated around the Ad Lib, the Scene and the Flamingo, was a photograph of 'some people who make London swing'. And there amongst the artists and photographers – Gerald Scarfe and David Bailey, Peter Blake and David Hockney – were a clutch of designers including the now established queen of women's fashion, Mary Quant, and the new kid on the block, Barbara Hulanicki. Less than a year on from the gingham dress, Biba was being publicly invited to join the top table. A couple of months later a feature ran in *Queen* magazine titled 'Society: The Index', which determined what was in and what was out in a range of categories that included everything from diseases to disc jockeys,

BIBA IS A MUST SCENE FOR THE SWITCHED-ON DOLLY-BIRD AT LEAST TWICE A WEEK

from gynaecologists to gyms. The list of boutiques that were looked upon with favour read: Countdown, Palisades, Furore, Bazaar, Biba, Foale & Tuffin, Maxine Leighton, Tony Armstrong.

The final seal of approval, both for Biba and for London, came a year after the *Telegraph* piece, when *Time* magazine in America ran a cover story anointing the capital as the city of the decade. 'As for the girls,' it pointed out, 'the most In shop for gear is Biba's boutique in Kensington, which is a must scene for the switched-on dolly-bird at least twice a week. Designer

Shop-manager Kim Willmot in one of the window seats at Kensington High Street – the window painting was by Antony Little.

Barbara Hulanicki, owner of Biba's, estimates that a typical secretary or shop girl, earning $31 a week, will spend at least $17 of it on clothing, which leaves her with a cup of coffee for lunch – but happy.'

By this point, as befitted a store with a growing national and international reputation, Biba had moved to larger premises, a former grocery known as Home & Colonial at 19–21 Kensington Church Street. The move to the new shop, in March 1966, was achieved in a carefully arranged PR stunt that saw the shop girls pushing rails of clothes up Abingdon Road and across Kensington High Street, passing on the way the buildings that would house the next two incarnations of the store. Meanwhile a van was pulling up in Kensington Church Street to allow the unloading of pot plants and yet more clothes by, amongst others, Cathy McGowan and Cilla Black. (Barbara repaid the favour to Cilla later that year by designing her costume for an appearance in pantomime as Little Red Riding Hood.) The photo-opportunity, proudly proclaiming a collective enthusiasm, reflected no more than the reality: this was a team and, away from the cameras, even the bank manager who had arranged the necessary funds was said to have been seen pushing a clothes rail along a pavement.

At 1,100 square feet, the new store was four times the size of Abingdon Road, giving more scope not only for an enlarged stock, but also for décor and design. The 'Cavern Club darkness' of Abingdon Road was retained, and many customers still responded to the 'feeling of boudoir', but there was a more dramatic sweep to the setting. 'She didn't want to sell,' points out designer Anthea Davies, 'she wanted to create theatre; she was always waxing lyrical about the twenties or thirties film stars.' Barbara herself explained her approach to decoration when talking about her own home: 'One's relationship with a room is, I've decided, rather like marriage. If you allow yourself to unlock all its secrets, it can become boring. Things get taken for granted. I like a room with a little mystery.' So successful was the Church Street store at creating mystery that by 1968 *Vanity Fair* was describing it as 'the most exotic shop in London'.

BOTTOM LEFT: *Packaging from stockings, 1966, with logo design by Antony Little, and (left) labels showing size, colour and price.*

RIGHT: *One of the drawings by Antony Little sold in Kensington High Street.*

Key to the appeal of the Biba stores was Barbara's ability to spot and to attract creative collaborators, one of the first of whom was Julie Hodgess. In 1965 Hodgess was just starting to establish herself as a wallpaper designer when Barbara 'saw some of her work and immediately knew that that was exactly what she wanted for her wild and way out shops.' A commission to re-do the walls at Abingdon Road was now followed by a similar invitation to decorate the new store, for

which she created a theme of red, aubergine and gold. Helping her print the paper on the first occasion had been Antony Little, who himself had aspirations to be a designer. Shortly before Church Street opened, he had painted the windows for Michael Rainey's boutique, Hung On You, in Cale Street, Chelsea, and he went on to do the same for the new Biba. He painted the name above the shop, and blacked out most of the windows with a design of his own making in gold and black; an adaptation of the design was used as a logo for bags and other printed materials, replacing the earlier cancelling-stamp motif.

The work that Little did for Biba reflected a growing taste in youth culture for the Art Nouveau of the late-nineteenth century. After many decades out of fashion, the free-flowing, organic writhing of Art Nouveau had gradually begun to make a comeback via a series of gallery exhibitions: Alphonse Muncha at the Victoria and Albert Museum in 1963, 'The Collection of Martin Battersby' at the Brighton Museum in 1964, and a touring exhibition 'Art Nouveau in Britain' in 1965. The tipping point came with the V&A's exhibition of Aubrey Beardsley in 1966, attracting a species of visitor that initially baffled at least one observer; looking back, George Melly wrote of the strange young people that surrounded him that: 'I believe now that I had stumbled into the presence of the emerging underground.'

Beardsley did indeed become something of a patron saint of the underground scene in London. His strong, sinuous drawings, his wilful breaking of taboos and his early death made him a proto-rock

icon to the generation of designers that created British psychedelia. Amongst them was Little, who, in addition to the windows, also did a series of drawings for sale as prints via Biba: 'I admire Beardsley,' he said at the time. 'His work has a tremendous sense of design and an acute sense of decoration. As designs – his drawings and paintings – they're perfect. The nearest thing to Beardsley is Greek architecture – everything perfectly controlled.' He went on to add that, although this obsession with Art Nouveau might seem as though it were backward-looking, it was actually very contemporary: 'The Beardsley feeling fits in very well with the general attitude for satire – a kickback against vagueness in art.' Julie Hodgess was another who admitted the influence; she described her wallpaper designs for Church Street as being 'like Aubrey Beardsley jungles'.

To Barbara, already instilled with an interest in the past by Aunt Sophie, the Art Nouveau revival was meat and drink: 'For me,' she said in 1967, 'Art Nouveau is never still, always convoluted, unlikely to be boring. Indoors, the elements of the style can produce real warmth and nostalgia, which I find bewitching, and, of course, it's all a trifle decadent.'

The enthusiastic embrace of Nouveau was confirmed later in 1966 when John McConnell devised a new logo for Biba. 'What happened,' he recalls, 'was that Barbara bought some cologne – frightful-smelling stuff – and she found a fake cut-glass bottle with a stopper, and said, "We'd better do a label for this cologne".' McConnell found a printer's mark in a Scandinavian type-book, adapted it, added the word 'Biba' in a typeface that echoed 'the 1890s style of the Liberty's department store' and produced a label. The swirly pattern, reminiscent of both Art Nouveau and Celtic knotwork, although it derived from neither, was subsequently revised and, over time, the existing typeface was replaced with a thinner, more sophisticated lettering devised by McConnell himself. But the essential concept remained, and the resulting logo became indelibly associated with Biba. It also became recognised as a design classic, though McConnell is quick to point out that its position derives from the success of the store: 'If Biba had failed in its first year, that mark wouldn't mean anything; it's only grown into its status because of what Biba did.'

Now firmly established as a key element in what felt like the cultural capital of the world, Biba became a stopping-off point for tourists, as the *Evening News* noted: 'Everyone under 30 coming to London made a beeline for Biba.' Celebrity visitors included Mia Farrow (who 'bought the worst dress in the shop'), Sharon Tate, Barbra Streisand, Sonny and Cher, Jack Nicholson and Yoko Ono, as well as Mick Jagger, first with Chrissie Shrimpton and then with Marianne Faithfull. (His other half in the Stones didn't shop there himself, but the influence was still felt, as Anita

BELOW LEFT: *The first version of what was to become the best-known Biba logo, designed by John McConnell, on a cologne bottle and (left) its more familiar incarnation.*

BELOW: *Biba staff in 1966, with (left to right): Suzanne Bates, Eleanor Powell, Rosie Young, Fitz, Eva Molnar, Dee Dee Wilde, Barbara, Susy Young, Kim Willmot.*

Pallenberg points out: 'Keith used to steal my clothes. He loved wearing my little Biba jackets on stage.')

Rosie Young, who worked with her twin sister, Susy, at Church Street, remembers the way that the staff took most of this in their stride: 'Whoever came to England came into Biba. So you saw all the film stars, all the famous people. The person who caused the most stir in my time was Brigitte Bardot – everyone came out from the back. She and Princess Anne were the two people who caused everyone to sit up.' Fabric designer Anthea Davies was working in the back room of the shop in the summer of 1966: 'One day I was in my little room. Next thing I knew Brigitte Bardot had walked in with her then husband, Günter Sachs, and was starting to strip down to her bra and pants, trying on clothes in my little room, because the changing room in the shop was communal, and she was very famous then. Max the accountant popped in to have a cup of tea, and he reeled backwards – there was Brigitte Bardot in her underwear.'

The biggest British film star to associate herself with Biba was Julie Christie, whose wardrobe for *Darling*, John Schlesinger's caustic, classic 1965 tale of Swinging London, came from the store, but there was home-grown talent as well. Madeline Smith was discovered whilst doing a summer job in Biba, and went on to appear in a string of celebrated horror films including *The Vampire Lovers* and *Theatre of Blood*, as well as modelling for the Biba

mail-order catalogues. Others, too, were whisked off from the store: 'Four of us from Biba were asked by a Frenchman to go and dance in a club in the South of France,' remembers Sarah Burnett, 'and so off we went. We were called Les Minis Anglaises or something like that. It was very innocent, just putting on records, but the four of us were recruited and went to work in a nightclub in the South of France. It was quite extraordinary.' Meanwhile shop assistant Dee Dee Wilde had to wait for Pan's People the following decade to make her name, taking happy memories with her: 'I met Raquel Welch once when she came in and demanded I remove my pink dress and sell it to her. I did.'

Most famous of all was the 15-year-old schoolgirl who became known as Twiggy. After her first attempt at a photo shoot with her future manager, Justin de Villeneuve, he took her home and they got talking: 'He asked me if I knew a shop called Biba. He said Biba did wonderful clothes and that they would suit me... [It] was a knockout. I'd never seen anything like it before. I loved the clothes, and I loved the dark mahogany screens everywhere.' Twiggy continued to wear Barbara's creations and became for many the most visible symbol of the waif-like ideal of a Biba girl.

The shift from the mod sensibility, articulated by the original logo, to the Art Nouveau feel of the Celtic mark was reflected in the clothes themselves. The new style, reflects Antony Little, was 'a mixture of thirties, Art Nouveau and even Pre-Raphaelite'.

BIBA

Biba was going beyond its early style of girlhood to offer a collective version of the same: a retreat not merely to the more innocent days of its individual customers but to those of society as a whole, developing its interest in Victoriana in a way that confused the less astute commentators of the time. The *Daily Mail* of 1967 had trouble reconciling Biba, 'a name synonymous with young, trend-setting fashion', with the décor of Barbara's own house that was 'decades apart in inspiration'.

While London fashion was still predominantly associated with primary colours, geometric shapes and op art, Biba was working to an entirely different agenda. A shopper of the time remembers the merchandise as 'slithery gowns in glowing satins, hats with black veils, shoes stacked for sirens,' whilst 'for real life there were raincoats to sweep the London pavements, t-shirts the colour of old maids' hats, dusky suede boots with long zippers.' The reference to the old-maid colours ('Auntie colours', as Barbara called them) is entirely appropriate; though Biba was still capable of producing bright clothes that didn't look adrift in the mainstream, there was a growing emphasis on purples and plums, blacks and browns that was heading down what appeared to be a backwater. 'There had always been a twenties air about Biba,' Twiggy later reflected, 'with the potted palms and bentwood hat stands; now the clothes were following suit and the hat stands were draped with feather boas.'

And yet the shop was still predominantly the preserve of the young: 'Old, in our view,' recalls shop manager Eleanor Powell, 'was anyone over 25.'

And an early attempt to sell a long skirt – in contravention of the mini standard – had been abandoned, according to Barbara, because it sold to 'the wrong people; 35-year-olds came in and bought it, who rather thought they were onto something. Actually, our girls in the shop, they liked it, but I think the boys didn't like it.' The inspiration was vintage but the ethos was still very much of the now, as Julie Hodgess emphasised: 'I love Barbara Hulanicki's clothes – most of my things are from her and I wear them a long time – even if it is a crime to be seen in last year's Biba. I'm glad that fancy dress has spread to the street. It's part of the exotic revival, much better to be even a bit ridiculous than boring.'

By now the national wave of optimism that had so inspired *Time* magazine and others was beginning to dissipate; the sad fact was that, after a feverish burst of activity, England no longer 'swung like a pendulum do'. Creativity was still riding high, but the devaluation of the pound in October 1967, combined with the simultaneous veto of British entry into the EEC by Charles de Gaulle – for the second time – had dented the self-belief of New Britain, taken the gloss off the veneer, and the shabbiness beneath was starting to show through. (With the advent of the midi skirt that winter, it was reported that hemlines were falling 'as swiftly as the pound sterling'.)

Aspects of the retro-chic espoused by Biba were becoming everywhere apparent. In 1968 a BBC1 repeat of the series *The Forsyte Saga*, previously seen only on the minority BBC2 channel, attracted eighteen million viewers to its recreation of a more comforting vision of Britain, and even the likes of *Petticoat* magazine were talking about 'the mad rush for Victoriana'. Meanwhile an independent American movie that had initially failed to make much of an impression in its homeland was taking off like gangbusters in the UK: *Bonnie & Clyde*, starring Warren Beatty and Faye Dunaway and set in a stylised fantasy version of the 1930s, was the hit of 1968, inspiring a welter of pieces in the fashion press about 'playing gangsters' and 'how to dress like a gangster's moll'.

The cultural trend was towards the past. 'People went up into their attics and rummaged in Granny's trunks to see what they could find,' reflects George Melly, adding wryly that the motto of the time was, to misquote Henry Ford: 'History is junk'. But while the Beatles were trumpeting their sense of irony by donning vintage military outfits for *Sgt Pepper*, Biba was playing its revivalism with a straight face: this wasn't kitsch but a sincere love of a style that had been unfashionable for too long – 'shopping without cynicism', as it has been called.

———————

Amongst the most significant additions to the range in the Church Street shop was the expansion from women's clothes to include a children's department. This was, of course, not unrelated to the fact that in June 1967 Barbara gave birth to a son, who was named Witold after his late grandfather. From the outset, she was clear about how this event fitted in with her design philosophy: 'I'm all for a child developing in an environment of strong colours,' she said. 'At four months Witold is in mauve; it harmonises with his Parma-violet cot cover.'

The same sense of definite colours was by now a hallmark of the shop as a whole. In December 1966 the basement was opened as a changing room and was decorated by Julie Hodgess, with gold ceiling tiles and magenta walls, while the staircase was done in a 'zinging tomato red'. The changing room itself was communal, an innovation that had started in Abingdon Road, and one of the few developments for which succeeding generations of women have shown no desire to thank Biba. Originating out of necessity, according to John McConnell – 'We couldn't afford to build cubicles.' – it was the first communal changing room in Britain and became a symbol of the egalitarian spirit of the age. Where Mary Quant was introducing 'cylindrical capsule-shaped changing cubicles', Biba had little more than a curtain. The new basement changing room was more accommodating, but it did nothing to ease the major problem of such shared facilities: the encouragement to shoplift.

Biba was far from unique in attracting shoplifters, but early on it acquired a reputation for being an easy touch, with its combination of reticent sales assistants and very low lighting (the poor light put paid to the experimental use of closed-circuit television). It was not unknown for customers to change while in the store and walk out in a new outfit altogether, leaving a discard pile behind. Interviewed in 1966, Barbara insisted that the situation was under control: 'It's getting much better – it was awful at first. But it's funny how [the shop girls] can spot someone who's going to do it the minute they walk in the shop.' As she implies, although store detectives were hired, the responsibility for monitoring nefarious visitors largely devolved on the sales force, with additional assistance from the back-of-house staff, as Anthea Davies recalls. 'On Saturdays I'd be hanging round the shop with Barbara, looking out for shoplifters; there was so much thieving going on.' She adds that she never apprehended anyone, but Eleanor Powell, who worked in a managerial capacity through the whole history of Biba, remembers confronting one customer who attempted to steal a pair of trousers, which he concealed under his flowing black cloak (not the most inconspicuous costume for a thief).

She followed him out of the store and demanded that he return the item, whereupon he hit her, knocking her out. She later had the satisfaction of seeing him sentenced to three months for assault.

Inevitably innocent bystanders were caught up in the somewhat amateur attempt at security, though it did nothing to dislodge their love of Biba: 'This girl came up to me and asked if she could look in my bag; she obviously thought I'd stolen something. I was absolutely mortified, I was really upset, because no one had ever accused me of stealing anything ever. It didn't stop me going, of course.'

*The pillow-packs designed
by John McConnell for the
mail-order catalogues.*

Many years later Fitz was to insist that the talk of wholesale looting was something of a myth, claiming that theft from Abingdon Road accounted for just 2 per cent of stock, a figure which might have been twice the national average, he said, but was still a long way behind the 18 per cent allegedly suffered at Way-In, the in-store boutique at Harrods. In any event, it was a price worth paying: 'Only the good things went. It was a choice of nailing stuff to the floor or selling it.' And, given the huge profitability of the shops, the problem was evidently within manageable proportions. For despite the theft, Biba continued to grow and by 1969 was claiming to have 'more turnover per square foot than any store in the world.'

Perhaps the greatest tribute to its success came from a rival, already established in Church Street. 'I felt extremely nervous when I heard that Biba was opening three doors away from my store,' recalled Lee Bender, founder of Bus Stop. 'I did not consider then the amount of passing trade it might generate for me. But when I arrived at 9 a.m. the next morning I could not believe my eyes, there was a queue outside my shop. The doors opened and the clothes ran out.'

Even so, there are some who – in hindsight at least – have seen the move from Abingdon Road, the very success of the new store, as being the beginning of the end: 'It was already sowing the seeds of its own ruin,' wrote Mary Furness. 'The name was painted up for everyone to see: it was becoming more popular and more famous by the minute.' More typical, however, was the view expressed by shop-girl Sarah Burnett that saw it as

natural growth: 'In Abingdon Road there was a sense of urgency, a sense of excitement because it was new. I think it was maturing when it went to Kensington Church Street.'

1966, the year of the move from Abingdon Road, also saw the start of expansion in other areas, the first of which was perhaps the least successful. Returning to Aunt Sophie's territory, and to the scene of her own college career, Barbara opened a

BIBA WAS BECOMING MORE FAMOUS BY THE MINUTE

small shop on Queen's Road, Brighton. It seemed like a natural development; apart from the personal associations, Brighton had long enjoyed a symbiotic relationship with London, most recently as the bank holiday resort of choice for the capital's mods, and the recreation of the Biba style – complete with dark interior, bentwood hat stands and wallpaper by Julie Hodgess – should have been welcomed.

In some quarters, indeed, it was an instant hit. 'Someone told us that Biba had opened up the road,' remembers journalist Lesley Garner, then a final year student at the University of Sussex, 'we just dropped everything and rushed there.' The name was already familiar to the more fashion-conscious of the students, who knew it from London, and were aware of the seismic shifts in society: 'We were the epitome of everything the sixties stood for: youth, glamour, right-

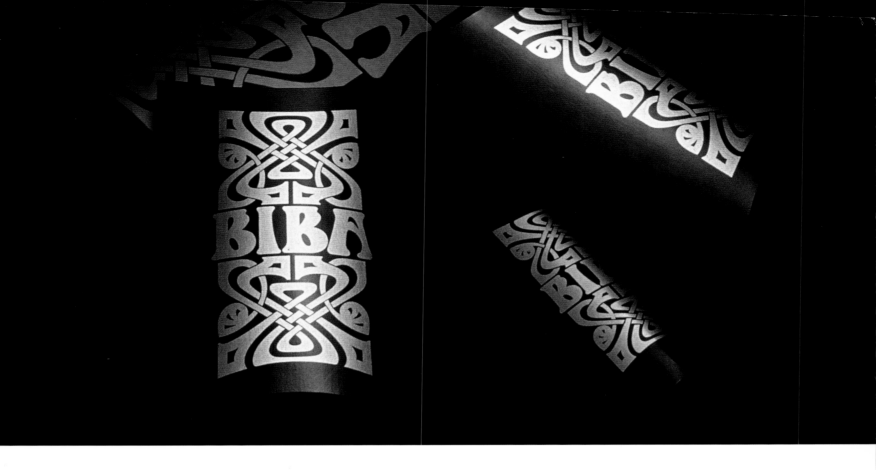

on political correctness, educational experimentation. We inhabited our brave new world by the sea wearing the first miniskirts and microscopic dresses.' It wasn't a feeling that was necessarily reciprocated by the Biba staff who went to work there: 'Brighton wasn't quite so much on the ball as London,' says Rosie Young. 'I remember one day a little old lady came in and said, "Is that what you call a bouquet?".'

Despite the enthusiasm with which the Brighton Biba was greeted by some, it lasted for just ten months, and by the end of the year it had closed. Barbara explained the failure of the project in terms of how it sapped energy from the main store in London: '[Church Street] involves so much personal attention, seeing that everything's in the right place and is working right and being looked after right. So it's a fag to have to break away from here and go down to Brighton to see that everything's alright, even once a fortnight.'

Eleanor Powell, who worked in the Brighton shop, adds that there were other problems attached to the venture: the novelty of a communal changing room didn't travel well beyond London, and – curiously – the sizes didn't correlate. Biba had, from the outset, specialised in small clothes, with sizes 8 and 10 proving the most popular; shoppers in Brighton, on the other hand, favoured size 14, and there were many who asked for a 16, which proved impossible: 'We didn't do 16s'. In later years, as the scale of the operation expanded, a wider range of sizes was made available, but in 1966 it was not considered economically viable to change production for the sake of one small shop.

A happier excursion saw the creation of a mini-boutique in the Hotel Post in Zermatt, Switzerland over the Christmas and New Year period in 1966. Then owned by an American, Karl Ivarsson, the hotel decided to adopt a Swinging London theme for the holiday season: a nightclub was created with go-go girls and nightly performances by The End, and a room was set aside to be fashioned into a replica Biba. Again Julie Hodgess designed a wallpaper – in the increasingly familiar combination of gold and black – while the hat stands were transplanted once more to stake their claim to a new territory. It was primarily a fun holiday for the staff who worked there for a couple of weeks each, but it did indicate the growing international status of Biba.

This was confirmed the following year, when a team of girls flew out to Brazil in August 1967 for a design competition being staged at the Sao Paulo fabric fair, and promptly won, seeing off opposition from the likes of Paco Rabanne and Rudi Gernreich.

The delegation on that occasion included, alongside Eleanor Powell and model Joanne Dingemans, the woman who many Biba insiders regard as having been absolutely essential to the success of the clothes: Annie Behr. She had studied alongside Barbara at Brighton and joined the company early on, cutting the clothes and bringing the sketches into reality. 'Annie was wonderful – she was the technician,' remembers one colleague. Behr hadn't studied pattern-cutting, and eschewed the standard technique of cutting on the flat in favour of working on a stand, but she had an instinctive flair for the art. 'It was her cuts,' says Powell, one of many to pay tribute to Behr's work, 'Barbara's designs were brilliant, but without Annie's cuts they would have looked very different.'

———

Despite these ventures away from home, the reality was that Biba was still essentially rooted in West London. There was increasing coverage in the national and international press, but for those unable to make it to Kensington, there were only the

withered remains of the mail-order service to provide access to the clothes, and then only when the odd media feature mentioned the address of the shop. And so it was decided to re-launch what had been the Postal Boutique under a new guise. The result was a series of mail-order catalogues, starting in April 1968, that followed no known precedent – 'Everything was different for the sake of being different,' noted one customer approvingly – and that took the message of Biba out across the country. In the process, they fixed the visual image of its style perhaps more than anything else in the history of the label.

John McConnell was given the task of producing something that would capture the spirit and ethos of Biba, in opposition to the existing standard of bulky catalogues (average weight: 5½ pounds) full of 'horrid drawings'. Barbara's instructions were to 'create the atmosphere of a magazine editorial', and he conceived a long, thin document – designed to fit through a standard letter-box without being creased – containing just eight garments, shown in highly stylised photographs. These were intended to evoke an aspirational image, so that a potential customer would respond on an emotional level: 'When I meet my boyfriend next Saturday evening, I want to look like that.' The pictures were taken by an impressive succession of photographers – Donald Silverstein, Hans Feurer, Helmut Newton, Sarah Moon and Harri Peccinotti – most of whom were then only just making their name, and featured side-lit studio shots that oozed glamour, partly, at least, because they were printed in duotone: 'We couldn't afford full-colour print.' Amongst the models were Madeline Smith, Stephanie Farrow, Marie Knopka,

3
Bonded crepe coat dress.
Dressingown collar tied at
the side with a bow. Long
narrow sleeves with split
opening at the wrist.
Colours navy or red.
Spotted square can be worn
at neck.
Price
£4·19·6

For rings, bracelets and
scarf see back page.

4
Narrowly cut waistcoat —
fully lined. Buttoned and
pocketed like the real thing,
teams up with front-pleated
skirt in honey coloured
heavy linen-like rayon.
Price together
£3·19·6

4b
The blouse (can be bought
separately) has jugglers'
sleeves and rounded collar.
The material is black and
white spotted
silky rayon crêpe
Price
£2·17·6

For rings, bracelets and
glasses see back page.

Quinilla, Elizabeth Bjorn Neilson, Donna Mitchell, Ingemari Johanson and Vicky Wise.

The slimness of the catalogues meant that only a handful of pieces were ever available, and they tended to be at the upper end of the Biba range. Even so, prices were still kept a reasonable level, so that a knit jumpsuit illustrated in the final catalogue was available for £9 19s 6d. At a time when the average non-manual wage for women had risen to £17 a week, this was still accessible, and it compared favourably with the 11 guineas that Jinty were asking for a wool jumpsuit, let alone the 18 guineas that it cost to buy one of Mary Quant's stretch satin versions of the same garment.

To run this new branch of the enterprise, Barbara called on the services of Tony Porter, husband of her sister Beatrice, who had recently returned from a job with ICI in Nigeria following the outbreak of the Biafran War. For him it was not an entirely obvious career move – 'It was a very low salary, threatened long hours and I knew absolutely nothing about fashion' – but he responded both to the allure of Biba and to the challenges it presented; Barbara thrived on the excitement of trying herself in new fields and her attitude encouraged others to do the same. A sorting machine was bought, punch-card operators employed, and the first catalogue launched with a barrage of publicity. The response was immediate and, despite the preparations, almost overwhelming: 'We were just swamped – we got three or four full sacks every morning, with literally hundreds, or even thousands of orders.'

Completing the service, and helping to distinguish it further from the existing mail-order companies, the clothes were despatched in distinctive black pillow-packs, complete with a gold Biba logo, designed by John McConnell. The intention was to head off disappointment if the service was interrupted so that even if 'they got this thing a month later than they had anticipated, their enthusiasm was rejuvenated.' Unfortunately, although they were certainly stylish, the boxes 'didn't stand up to the post, and a lot of dresses went missing; about a month later we'd get a mangled box back.'

The mail-order operation was theoretically separate from the shop (though its supplies were sometimes plundered to provide stock for the store), which caused further problems for customers: 'I bought a beautiful tweed trouser suit, but there was something wrong with the trousers and I had to go and take them back. And they were very awkward in the shop, said it was mail order, nothing to do with them and they couldn't do an exchange.'

Despite these logistical difficulties, the catalogues were an enormous success, taking Biba to an even greater market and, maybe even more importantly, spreading the look of what Barbara referred to as 'the Biba dolly', the idealised consumer of her products: her hair was 'a halo of golden ringlets, her cheeks were hollowed by brown powder, and her lips stained with sepia lipstick. The thin line of her brows framed her sparkly blue eyes … She was so young that all those Auntie colours that I had hated when I was young looked new on her.' Still working

without the benefit of advertising, Biba had hitherto relied on newspaper and magazine spreads to publicise Barbara's vision in print; now there was a direct medium of communication established, and the iconic images that were created have remained – along with the later series of posters – the most enduring face of Biba.

The result, according to McConnell, was to enhance the status of Biba in its heartlands. 'The idea was that this would enable people who couldn't get to London to buy a Biba frock,' he says. 'In actual fact, it increased sales in the south of England, amongst people who could get to the shop.' So marketable did the catalogues appear that there were plans to expand them internationally, and Shirley Shurville – who had recently arrived at Biba from Mary Quant and who had extensive international connexions – made initial contact with J. C. Penney to take them to America, but the discussions failed to come to fruition.

In total, six catalogues were produced, but towards the end things 'started to go badly wrong': the commitment became too great, the supplies of fabric began to get log-jammed and complaints were aired on TV and appeared in newspaper consumer columns. The mail-order department was wound up in the summer of 1969 and Porter found himself signing 'about three thousand cheques to send all the money back to the girls who wouldn't get their dresses.' Any sadness, however, was tinged by the appearance of a new challenge that took a much higher priority: the move to even more substantial premises, and the resultant transformation of Biba from boutique to department store.

OH, YOU PRETTY THINGS

LOOK AT YOUR CHILDREN, SEE THEIR FACES IN GOLDEN RAYS

DAVID BOWIE: 'OH, YOU PRETTY THINGS' DAVID BOWIE

The new store was a former Cyril Lord carpet showroom on the north side of Kensington High Street (numbers 124–126), a double-fronted property with around 9,000 square feet of retail space. When it opened on 15 September 1969 it marked a major expansion of interest for the company: women's clothes were, of course, still the core of the business, but now they were joined by wallpaper and paint, cutlery and crockery, soft furnishings (everything from Biba lamps to pink satin sheets), even statues. What had begun as a cheap, streetwise version of couture was spreading rapidly into lifestyle, creating a total look that was thematically unified and colour coordinated.

The clothes were still, for the most part, comfortably affordable – 'We are providing something of the glamour and glitter of a former era, but at down-to-earth prices,' explained Fitz – but now there was an additional element in the form of the Gallery Collection. Drawing on the same styles and feel of the characteristic Biba look, the Gallery garments were made from better quality materials, came in even fewer numbers than the standard pieces, and cost around twice as much: a velvet trouser suit, for example, cost 17 guineas, a silk blouse 12 guineas, and a full-length fake fur coat, 65 guineas. The new field was upmarket evening wear – sequined, sophisticated frocks – and it wasn't long before the

pieces were being worn not just by teenagers on TV, but by more mature women at social events: when April Ashley opened her restaurant, April & Desmonds, in Knightsbridge in 1970, she was widely photographed in a Biba evening dress.

There was also a menswear department on a mezzanine floor above the children's section at the back, a bold if ultimately unsuccessful attempt to broaden the appeal. The competition for the men's fashion market in London was by now highly developed and Biba was joining the race too far behind to make a real impact. Barbara was so firmly established as a women's designer that, while cushions and carpets were seen as a logical sideways extension of the business, menswear simply wasn't, and a company that was dominated by women failed to find an appropriate design ethos – lacking the intuitive genius that had become Biba's hallmark, the clothes looked laboured, and the quality was unimpressive.

Preparations for the new store were hurried and chaotic, with just a six-week period to make the premises ready for the move. Julie Hodgess was again asked to design the interior, including an elegant Edwardian environment for the Gallery, but

RIGHT: *The staircase at Kensington High Street, designed by Julie Hodgess, leading up to the Gallery.*

LEFT: *Part of the Conservatory area on the ground floor at Kensington High Street, designed by Antony Little, using windows from St Paul's School.*

RIGHT: *Promotional photo shoot for Biba's children's range.*

the pressures of time inevitably brought others into the process, including Antony Little, who worked on the changing rooms and 'a curious area that looked rather Venetian; I think it was meant to be Gothic, but in the end it looked more Venetian.' His utilisation of wooden panelling and stained glass from the nearby St Paul's School – which was scheduled for demolition – helped remove any trace of the atmosphere of the Cyril Lord days.

The design of the children's department, meanwhile, saw the involvement for the first time of the team of Whitmore-Thomas. Steve Thomas had already done some occasional small jobs for Biba, but the invitation to work on the High Street shop prompted him to form a partnership with Tim Whitmore, whom he had met at the Chelsea School of Art, and to begin an association that was to transform the image of the company and culminate in the design of Big Biba.

This new era of Biba saw the introduction of the peripheral merchandise that was to become so important in spreading the brand name. Back in 1966, a calendar and a diary had been produced for the following year, but this was a low-key affair compared to the plethora of products that spilled out of the High Street store. Suddenly there were address books, diaries, watches, passport holders, cigarette lighters and more, all bearing the logo, all proclaiming the owner of the item to be a participant in the Biba experience. And they were all wildly popular, the simple black-and-gold identity rendering them instantly recognisable and desirable.

Ever-more adventurous diversification was undertaken, including – amongst the projects that never materialised – plans for Biba cigars and cigarettes. An upmarket, re-launch of the mail-order catalogue offering made-to-measure outfits was also proposed, as well as a low-cost diffusion line to be called Thomasina. Most spectacular of all was the concept of the Biba car. The brief, as outlined by Fitz, was to produce a vehicle that would cost the same as a Mini but would have greater accelerating power. Responding to this specification, Whitmore-Thomas got as far as creating the plans for a wedge-shaped car, complete with voluminous ash-trays and a set of matching luggage specifically designed to fit perfectly in the boot. Sadly, it never got beyond the drawing board, overtaken by events in the expanding Biba empire.

Despite these extra-curricular activities, the biggest hits of the period were the Biba boots –

high-heeled, knee-high footwear that came in suede and in canvas and boasted an array of colours: pink, mauve, dusty blue and more. 'Nearly every girl had a pair of these Biba boots,' remembers hair stylist Trevor Sorbie, then living in Essex, 'they were so popular.' The continually evolving range encouraged repeat visits: 'That excited us: we went every week. And the word got around … they were so cheap.' Tony Porter, who had moved from mail order to the store, also recalls the popularity of the items: 'There was an absolute fight when there was a delivery. The lorry would pull up in the little street behind the back and girls would be waiting there to see it coming and then run round to be the first in the queue.' Barbara later wrote that 75,000 pairs of the boots were sold in the first three months.

So ubiquitous had the name of the company become that the expression 'Biba boots' was in danger of losing its unique status and becoming applied generically to the style rather than the product. Similarly the idea of the Biba top or the Biba t-shirt – one of Barbara's early designs featuring a tight-fitting body with high armholes and a drawstring – was spreading to other manufacturers looking for slipstream sales. In this latter instance, Biba was obliged to go to the High Court in 1972 to get an injunction against Stratford Investments Ltd for breach of copyright on the use of the term 'Biba t-shirt', and won a judgement that is still cited as a precedent in case law.

The scale of Biba's success in Kensington High Street was quite extraordinary. It was attracting 100,000 visitors a week – up to 30,000 of them on a Saturday – and could claim an annual turnover of more than £200 per square foot, compared to the £75 achieved by John Lewis and the £50 of an average department store. Meanwhile, there was also a growing critical recognition of Barbara's designs: in 1971 an exhibition at the Victoria and Albert Museum entitled 'Fashion: An Anthology' included two of her pieces – a skirt suit and a girl's dress, both in black velvet – that had been donated by Cecil Beaton, marking the first appearance of Biba clothes in a museum. And there was approval, too, from more orthodox quarters; when the Business pages of the *Observer* looked back at the stars of the sixties economy, it included Barbara as the only woman in the company of Sir Lew Grade, Richard Seifert, Sir John Cohen, Lord Stokes and Jim Slater.

There were those at the time who doubted the wisdom of the expansion from Church Street, and there are still many habitués of the early shops who regard it as being a step too far away from the original vision, but the sales figures were a triumphant vindication of the development. As the white heat of Harold Wilson's technological revolution began to cool, and Britain sought reassurance from semi-detached, suburban Mr Heath, Biba was going from strength to strength.

Up until the move to Kensington High Street, Biba had been operating as a purely private concern with Fitz as a sole trader. Fiercely protective of Barbara and her interests, he had nurtured the seeds of the company and seen them start to grow. Biba in the sixties was based not only on Barbara's instinctive grasp of the emerging identity of young women – financially independent, sexually confident and sartorially expressive – but also on Fitz's almost street-trader approach to business. In terms of both physique and character, he was a big man who seemed to revel in playing the role of Biba's bouncer, and in doing deals that took him to the edge: he would arrange a delivery of clothes for Thursday with payment due within seven days, displaying an absolute confidence that the entire stock would be sold on Saturday, thus giving him the cash flow to pay the bill.

For suppliers, such as IVO Prints Ltd of West London, who printed fabrics for Biba, he could be a nightmare client, albeit one who warranted respect: 'He was a good businessman, but you could print and print and print and he wouldn't pay. One time he said that it was all wrong, so he sent it all back. Then we found out we didn't print it at all – it was some other printer they went to and they made a mistake.' But there was always Barbara to smooth over such difficulties: 'She was marvellous.' Even those who worked closer to the heart of Biba had problems: 'One of the difficulties was getting paid,' says Antony Little. 'The whole time I used to have to go round there and sit in the waiting room, trying to see Fitz to get some money out of him. He was a very nice fellow, but getting paid was quite something.'

Meanwhile the money being generated by the shops themselves was almost literally overflowing. 'There were Edwardian jam-pots and Victorian urns and things everywhere, stuffed with money,' remembers Anthea Davies. 'Real cash. Money floating everywhere – it was absolute chaos. And if you wanted anything, Barbara said "Help yourself".

And you'd take the money. It was very, very free.' In such circumstances, mistakes were bound to be made: 'Every two hours or so one of the girls would come out from the office and collect the money in a Biba bag,' recalls Rosie Young. 'One day a girl came in to return a feather boa – it was the wrong colour or something – but instead of the bag with the new boa, she was given the bag with all the money in it. So she walked out. Funnily enough, I met her at a dinner party afterwards and she told the story. That's how terribly haphazard and very casual the whole thing was.'

THERE WERE EDWARDIAN JAM-POTS AND VICTORIAN URNS AND THINGS EVERYWHERE, STUFFED WITH MONEY

The fact was that, despite Fitz's relish for a shrewd deal, Biba was not orientated towards money. Its currency was creativity, combined with unreasonably long hours, and those who worked there found themselves swept away by the enthusiasm and devotion: 'We were all very badly paid,' says Daphne Bewes, who spent seven years with the company, 'but actually we would have worked for nothing. Barbara and Fitz's genius was the fact that we would have all worked for nothing. Because it was such fun.' That word 'fun' is a recurring theme in the reminiscences of the inner circle of Biba; it was an adventure, a life of spontaneity, glamour and excitement. 'Barbara would say to me on Friday, "Oh, let's go

*The refurbished children's
department at Kensington
High Street, sketched (left) by
Malcolm Bird, and as built
and painted (right) by Bird
and Romey McDonald.*

somewhere." And we'd go to the airport and see
what plane was going to Istanbul or somewhere,
come back Tuesday, having gone round all the
markets and found things.'

And out of this spirit of fun there came profits at a
level for which other retailers would have scarcely
dared dream. But the taste for empire-building was by
now in the blood, and shortly after the expansion into
Kensington High Street – which had only been
financed by a massive sale at Church Street – a deal
was struck that would transform the company entirely.

─────────

Back in 1966 Barbara had been asked if she wanted
to venture into make-up as Mary Quant had recently
done, to which she replied: 'Oh yes, I'd like to do
anything really.' But then she added the caveat that:

'The thing is that with make-up you need fantastic
distribution. You couldn't do it through one shop.'

In fact, when the Biba cosmetics range was
introduced, it was indeed only stocked in the one
shop. But the potential was apparent from the
outset: unlike the clothes sales that were based on a
rapid turnover and that were bulky and awkward to
transport, make-up was compact and enduring; all
that was needed was that 'fantastic distribution'. In
December 1969 the era of Fitz as sole trader came
to an end with the formation of Biba Ltd, a new
company in which Barbara and Fitz held 25 per cent
of the stock, the remainder being split between the
chain-store Dorothy Perkins, the merchant bank
Charterhouse, Japhet & Thomasson and Dennis
Day Ltd, a garment manufacturer.

Of these, the key player was Dorothy Perkins,
who held 35 per cent of the shares. Founded by
Samuel Farmer (and named after the popular
rambling rose), the chain was still, in 1969, a family
business, run by Alan Farmer and his son, Ian, both
of whom seemed enthusiastic and keen to preserve
the spirit of Biba. What they brought to the party
was both the finance needed to keep the High Street
premises afloat and, just as importantly, a network
of over 300 hundred stores nationwide. The interest
was not in the clothes – their typical customer was
an older, more staid woman and would scarcely
have known what to do with Biba's increasingly
vampish outfits – nor even in the shop itself. Ian
Farmer had gone on record in 1966 saying that
'Kensington is a darned awkward area … I wouldn't
take a shop there tomorrow.' But the cosmetics
offered a mutually beneficial way forward: to

modernise Dorothy Perkins by attracting a younger customer base, and to give Biba the national, and ultimately international, platform it sought.

Accordingly, in April 1970, the press were invited to the launch of Biba cosmetics at a tea dance, complete with a Palm Court trio and a huge cake ('a voluptuous Mae West figure lying on a bed of marzipan red roses') designed by Malcolm Bird, who had recently re-worked the children's department. It was an incongruously sedate situation for what was such a radical collection. For while the colours were familiar enough to Bibaphiles, they were startling in the context of make-up: dark brown, plum, mulberry, mahogany, even black – this wasn't what was expected of lipstick and eye shadow in 1970. And if Barbara had had her way, the palette would have been even more extreme: 'She did have some strange ideas; she

wanted green foundation, but fortunately they couldn't make it. We ended up with yellow foundation, there was no pink in it at all.'

The resulting proto-Goth vision added a whole new dimension to what was still mistakenly seen as a delicately nostalgic style: 'Biba wasn't romantic,' protests photographer Sarah Moon. 'It was more poisoned than that. Remember they did black lipstick.' When the range was rolled out into the Dorothy Perkins stores across the land, it created a vision that came as something of a shock to a generation of tank-top-wearing provincial boys: 'The lads just thought we looked like ghouls!' It was a long way from the Avon lady to the Biba dolly. Nonetheless the small black-and-gold pots and bottles, replicating the feel of an old-style apothecary, combined with the exaggerated false eyelashes, won a legion of new enthusiasts: 'There

The display units that were unleashed upon the country were purpose-built by Whitmore-Thomas in the warehouse facilities at Bracknell that Dorothy Perkins had made available. Constructed in black and decorated with mirrors, the units had harder, geometric lines that suggested a shift from Nouveau to Art Deco, and came complete with detailed instructions of the exact arrangement of all the contents: nothing was to be left to chance or interpretation. Biba was by now one of the most recognisable brands in the country and Barbara was determined to keep a tight grip on its every manifestation, no matter how trivial it might seem. 'She was the nearest thing to a genius I've ever come across,' says Daphne Bewes, 'totally single minded and a perfectionist. I remember once I spent thousands of pounds on stock-box labels, and they came back wrong. The only people who were going to see them were the people in the factory and the warehouseman, but they had to be altered. That's what she was like.'

This attention to detail became even more important for the next phase of the expansion planned with the funds that had become available. In 1971 Biba cosmetics, displayed on identically themed stands and complete with a Biba girl from London, opened in landmark stores around the world: Au Printemps in Paris, Fiorucci in Milan, Tekano in Japan (owned by Mitsubishi), Bloomingdale's in New York and some 18 or so outlets of the Judy's chain in California. These were virtually all virgin territories, with the exception of France, where a small selection of clothes had been sold through the Prisunic stores in 1968.

had never been anything like that before, in terms of the range and the variation. I saw it in Leeds, a big circular display with masses and masses of different coloured eye shadows that you'd never ever seen before, different colour lipsticks, little pots of lip gloss.' And in 1972 Biba followed the success of its cosmetics with Britain's first-ever range of make-up explicitly aimed at black women, an admirable if less durable enterprise: 'I'm not sure we got it terribly right,' reflects Daphne Bewes, 'but at least we tried.'

As for America, there had been only tentative forays, with the unrealised expansion of the mail-order catalogues, and a licence to sell sewing patterns through the McCall's Pattern Company. Even so, Biba products had been available in New York in the mid-sixties for those who sought them out, principally in Norma Kamali's boutique. Then working for an airline, Kamali had become a regular visitor to London and had got into the habit of taking clothes and music back to supply Anglophile friends in need of a fix. 'Finally,' she says, 'the demand was so great I opened a store in the basement of a group of brownstones in Manhattan.' By 1967 she had begun supplementing the stock with the first fruits of her own career as a designer, but the magic of Biba continued to provide inspiration. Meanwhile, a proposal to open Biba's own retail outlet in New York had been mooted, and suitable premises had even been found, but the funds weren't available and the plan came to nothing.

Now, with the cosmetics exposure in Bloomingdale's, combined with the arrival of Biba fabrics in Macy's and extensive coverage in *Seventeen* magazine, the attention was attracted of Bergdorf Goodman, one of the most prestigious and established department stores in New York. Two other British retailers – the Delman Shoe Salon and the antique dealers Mallett's – already had outlets in the store, and in February 1971 a mini-boutique was opened at Bergdorf's. This featured not merely the cosmetics but also boots, t-shirts, hats, feather boas, jewellery and accessories, a range of products with prices ranging from 75 cents to $75, all set within as close a reproduction of the original as was possible, complete with hat stands for authenticity. Again the display units were manufactured in Britain and flown out together with the stock – which is where the problems began. Having been held up at the airport, while – allegedly – frantic phone calls were made to the right underworld figures to allow entry, the mirrored centre-piece display unit then proved unable to withstand the rigours of a heavily air-conditioned New York department store; overnight the block-boards contracted, shattering every one of the hundreds of pieces of glass. A last-minute rush to cut and fix a new set of mirrors was achieved only just in time for the formal opening.

A further challenge came when Bergdorf Goodman offered eight windows on Fifth Avenue continuing round the corner on to 59th Street, for a display to celebrate the arrival of the new concession. By any standards, it was a fabulous opportunity but, as Steve Thomas points out, 'There was no tradition of Biba windows.' With the brief and minor exception of Brighton, this was the only time in the history of the company that a window display was prepared.

The venture was seen by some as an unlikely marriage between 'New York's 70-year-old citadel of elegance and London's high priestess of young fashion,' but Bergdorf Goodman were enthusiastic about 'the tremendous creative talent of Barbara Hulanicki and the business acumen of Stephen Fitz-Simon' and celebrated the rise of Biba as 'something of a miracle in modern retailing'. And the interest and sales generated clearly repaid their faith. The mini-Biba was a popular feature in the store and continued through to 1972, when it was overtaken by events at home.

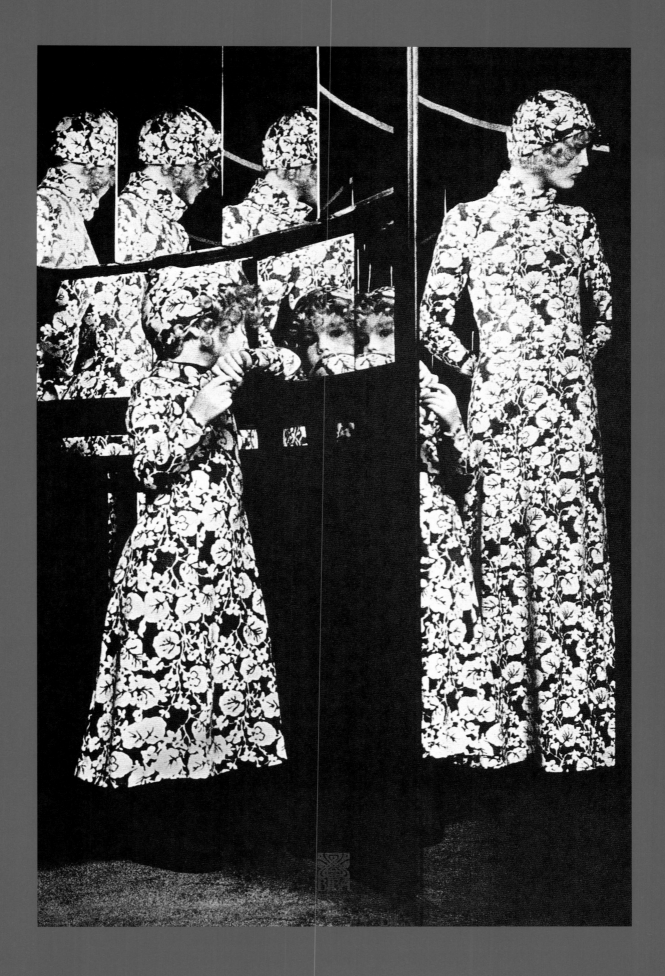

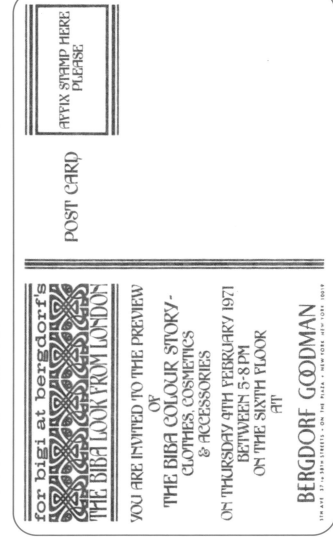

for bigi at bergdorf's

THE BIBA LOOK FROM LONDON

YOU ARE INVITED TO THE PREVIEW
OF
THE BIBA COLOUR STORY-
CLOTHES, COSMETICS
& ACCESSORIES

ON THURSDAY 4TH FEBRUARY 1971
BETWEEN 5-8 PM
ON THE SIXTH FLOOR
AT

BERGDORF GOODMAN

5TH AVE 57 to 58TH STREETS • ON THE PLAZA • NEW YORK NEW YORK 10019

POST CARD

AFFIX STAMP HERE PLEASE

The seeds of these events in turn lay mainly in the shift in the ownership of the company that had occurred in October 1970. Less than a year on from the creation of Biba Ltd, one of the original partners, Dennis Day had pulled out. 'The idea was that they were going to do the manufacturing,' says Shirley Shurville, 'but they soon realized that they couldn't cope with our quick turn-around; they were much more geared towards normal wholesale.' A realignment of the stock left Barbara and Fitz still holding 25 per cent, Charterhouse Japhet with 5 per cent and the remaining 70 per cent in the hands of Dorothy Perkins, effectively making Biba a subsidiary of that company. For now, it was working perfectly – 'they absolutely backed us to the hilt' – and undoubtedly the proceeds of a quarter-share of such a profitable enterprise were considerable for the managing director and creative director (as Fitz and Barbara now were).

These financial arrangements would come back to haunt Biba in the Derry & Toms years, but in the meantime there were other, more immediate, threats to face.

*Postcard invitation to the
press-launch of Biba in
Bergdorf Goodman, designed
by Whitmore-Thomas, 1971.*

May Day in 1971 fell on a Saturday, and to mark the international celebration of working class solidarity, the Angry Brigade planted a bomb in the basement at Biba.

The first phone-warning was received mid-afternoon and was summarily dismissed by the girl answering the call. At 3.30 p.m. a second warning was issued: 'You have only five minutes before the bomb goes off.' The tone was by now very panicked. 'At first,' said Fitz, 'I thought the caller was a crank but then I decided to take it seriously as there were about 5,000 people in the store, most of them women and children.' The store security officer, John Evans, later explained: 'I got the customers out to safety and then went downstairs into the basement to see what I could find. As I opened the stockroom door there was a violent explosion.' He was slightly injured, but fortunately he was the only casualty in an incident that could have had far more serious consequences. As it was, the damage was almost entirely confined to property: 'Half the basement was demolished. There were bits of hat stands all over the place.'

One of those there at the time remembers the chaos of the day. 'Someone said, "The shop is closing, will you please get out in the street as soon as possible." And of course everyone was screaming and at the same time stuffing things up their jumpers, pinching stuff like mad. There was one girl next to me having complete hysterics, flinging her arms around and saying, "Oh my God, oh my God, we're all going to die." And as she was doing this big drama thing, she was stuffing loads of things into her bag.'

It was one of the more unlikely episodes in the history of Biba. At the time the renewed war in Ireland had yet to spread to the mainland, bombings were far from commonplace, particularly in public places, and terrorism had yet to become a fact of life for Londoners. The first acknowledged Angry Brigade action had been a bomb that failed to explode outside Paddington Green police station in May 1970, with the most famous attack coming in the following January with two explosions at the house of the Employment Minister, Robert Carr. A series of bombings over an eighteen-month period were, so it was claimed, carefully targeted: 'Fascism and oppression will be smashed – Embassies, High Pigs, Spectacles, Judges, Property...' read an early Angry Brigade statement.

THERE WERE BITS OF HAT STANDS ALL OVER THE PLACE

Which raises the question: Why Biba? No other shop had been, or was ever to be, attacked by the group, and Biba didn't readily spring to mind as a symbol of 'fascism and oppression'. Indeed for many of its customers it was seen to be mounting the barricades itself: 'On the surface Biba's concern with fashion might have seemed suspiciously establishment, part of the problem, rather than the solution,' recalled Catherine Ross, one of those attracted by the mail-order catalogues. 'But to our 14-year-old eyes there was absolutely no doubt at all that Biba was "on our side" ... the Biba catalogues look[ed] far more subversive and potentially dangerous than other more overtly revolutionary publications like *Black Dwarf*.'

The Angry Brigade itself issued a press release, known as Communiqué #8, to *The Times* to explain the rationale behind the bombing.

```
IF YOU'RE NOT BUSY BEING BORN, YOU'RE BUSY
BUYING.
    All  the  sales  girls  in  the  flash
boutiques  are  made  to  dress  the  same  and
have  the  same  make-up,  representing  the
1940s.  In  fashion  as  in  everything  else
capitalism  can  only  go  backwards - they've
nowhere  to  go - they're  dead.
    The  future  is  ours.  Life  is  so  boring
there  is  nothing  to  do  except  spend  all
our  wages  on  the  latest  skirt  or  shirt.
    Brothers  and  Sisters,  what  are  your  real
desires?  Sit  in  the  drugstore,  look
distant,  empty,  bored,  drinking  some
tasteless  coffee?  Or  perhaps  BLOW  IT  UP  or
BURN  IT  DOWN.  The  only  thing  you  can  do
with  modern  slave-houses  -  called
boutiques  -  is  WRECK  THEM.  You  can't
reform  profit  capitalism  and  inhumanity.
Just  KICK  IT  TILL  IT  BREAKS.
    REVOLUTION.
```

Ignoring the critique of Biba's fashion sense (it was hard to believe that Barbara's fondness for retro was really the motivation), Scotland Yard pointed immediately to the attack being an attempt to appeal to radical feminists: 'way-out militant women on the fringes of the "Women's Lib" movement, but not connected with any organised group.' The connexion between the Angry Brigade and the Women's Liberation Movement had, the police stated, been under investigation for some months.

This claimed association with the more militant wing of early British feminism was not as implausible as it might now appear. One of the first public manifestations of the women's movement in the States had been a demonstration at the 1968 Miss America contest in Atlantic City, denouncing a culture based on the idea that 'women must be young, juicy, malleable – hence age discrimination and the cult of youth.' Suitably inspired, British feminists greeted the arrival of the Miss World contest at the Royal Albert Hall in November 1970 by throwing flour, stink bombs and smoke bombs to disrupt the proceedings inside the venue. This was little more than rag-week street theatre, but more worryingly a BBC Outside Broadcast van was blown up by a real bomb, in an attack whose authorship was never identified.

Amongst those who were concerned by this development in the struggle for women's rights was Erin Pizzey, who says she became even more alarmed when she heard suggestions within the movement of further attacks: 'I said that if you go on with this – they were discussing bombing Biba – I'm going to call the police in, because I really don't believe in this.' When she did indeed inform the police, she found herself obliged to leave the group in which she was participating, and instead went off to found the first refuge for the victims of domestic violence, beginning a campaign to force that issue on to the political agenda.

In the charged atmosphere of the time, the activities of the Angry Brigade were seen by many within the counter-culture as being effectively the most radical expressions of the war against straight society. The Christmas edition of *International Times* declared 1971 to be 'The Year of the Angry Brigade', whilst both *Oz* and *Frendz* magazine produced Angry Brigade issues late in the year, all of them subsequent to the Biba bombing. The group's ideological link with feminism was not obvious (the very first Angry Brigade communiqué had opened 'Dear Boss', in deliberate echo of Jack the Ripper, the most notorious woman-killer in British history), and it is striking that no statement issued after Communiqué #8 referred to the Biba bomb, as though it had been some kind of aberration, but it is just as significant that the attack did nothing to damage the reputation of the Angry Brigade as the shock troops of alternative Britain. Indeed the *Guardian* even argued that Biba should see it as 'some kind of macabre tribute' that anarchists

should single it out in order 'to protest the rising tide of capitalist female deco-decadence'.

The fact was that there were many on the left who had a strong ideological objection to Biba. It may have been the creation of a woman, its management structure may have been almost exclusively female, and it may have inspired feelings of empowerment and liberation amongst those who shopped there, but the 'objective reality' was that all the above were the victims of an industry designed to exploit women, to subjugate them and to lure them into consumerism. In the confused quasi-Marxist rhetoric of the times, Biba was the enemy. It was too successful, too visible, too seductive.

The depth of this hatred was nowhere better expressed than in the gloating coverage given by the left press to the campaign for union recognition within the Biba workforce. A piece on

Barbara in December 1969, wearing the maxi-waistcoat shown on page 139.

In the seventies, trade union culture was still dominated by masculine, manual labour and had difficulty finding a home in the big single stores in the West End, with their rapid turnover of predominantly young, female staff. Following a heavily publicised dispute with Foyle's, however, the shop-workers' union, USDAW, was enthusiastic when it was approached in 1972 by girls from Biba dissatisfied with their conditions of work and pay; none of the big retailers in Kensington High Street were unionised at that point, and Biba – already looking to expand into the Derry & Toms building – could well be the first domino to fall.

The women on the shop floor at Biba had never been particularly well paid, and *Spare Rib's* summary of the situation in Kensington High Street reflects the reality for those at the bottom: 'For an eight hour day, five days a week plus three-and-a-half hours at the weekend, their take-home pay was £11.15 and the only perk offered to staff is a one-third discount on any item over 50p. Holidays average out to one full day's paid holiday per month, and only one half-hour break is allowed during the whole working day.' What was missing from this description was a recognition that low pay was a general problem of the retail trade, and that there was an intangible, value-added benefit of being a Biba girl: there was the sense of belonging and of status that it brought. 'You'd really feel proud to get on a bus to go home in your Biba outfit, because everyone knew you worked there,' remembers one, whilst another points out that 'to work there was special; I got a big buzz that I worked for Biba.'

the subject in the feminist journal *Spare Rib*, for example, which was written by Felix Dennis – erstwhile defendant in the *Oz* trial and later the founder of *Maxim* magazine – deliberately and gleefully even referred back to the bombing of a year earlier with its headline 'Angry Brigade Mk. II Hits Biba'. The truth was less extreme and certainly less incendiary.

Shop workers have traditionally always been amongst the least unionised of all groups in Britain.

Bob White was then the Membership Secretary of the Eastern Division of USDAW, called in to assist the negotiations, and he is quick to pay tribute to the family spirit: 'Biba was a close-knit community; they all got on well.' The problems, according to White, started when new offices opened in Westbourne Grove in February 1972 away from the store, a move that divided the community between the core management staff on the one hand, and the shop workers on the other. Communication began to break down and those in the store no longer felt part of the team. Several months of stand-off followed between Fitz, not temperamentally a union supporter (he was said to be 'livid' about the *Spare Rib* articles), and the shop girls, led by a woman named Aina Vasilevskis and supported by USDAW, until in February 1973 the issue was resolved and a union branch was formed, with Vasilevskis elected as the first chairwoman. It was a close-run thing, remembers White, 'An eleventh hour decision; it all got called off when they gave in to our demands. The placards were all ready to go.'

Despite the struggle to be born, the union proved to be a model of cooperation in an era not noted for cordial relations between management and workforce in Britain. 'It was probably the best branch I ever had,' testifies Bob White. 'It was an open door; I never had to make an appointment to see Fitz. It was incredible.' The strength of the new structure was evidenced when things started to go wrong for the firm a couple of years later, and it became clear that Barbara and Fitz were seen as being on the same side as the shop workers against the forces trying to destroy the Biba family: 'At one point,' it was reported, 'a deputation approached Fitz-Simon and asked whether it would help if they staged a work-in.'

Meanwhile, as the union issue was being satisfactorily resolved, the bomb scares escalated. Although Biba was never again the target of a bomb after May Day 1971, the experience was so traumatic that every threat had to be taken seriously. Some were genuinely threatening – as the Provisional IRA began to wage its war on the streets of London – while others were hoaxes by glory-seekers and bandwagon-jumpers (Barbara remembers a call from the Guerrillas of Great Britain, a group heard of neither before nor since), but all resulted in the disruptions and inconveniences that became so much

> YOU'D REALLY FEEL PROUD TO GET ON A BUS TO GO HOME IN YOUR BIBA OUTFIT BECAUSE EVERY-ONE KNEW YOU WORKED THERE

a feature of life in the seventies. One customer who was caught up in such a scare recalls the incident as having a positive side: 'I was inside a changing room and was handed a robe to cover myself by one of the salespeople – it meant I had to wait around for the all clear to go back inside to get my own clothes. As odd as this sounds, that was a great time because the people employed by Biba were wonderful and turned what might have been a very unhappy experience into a pleasant one.'

CABARET

WE HAVE NO TROUBLES HERE – HERE LIFE IS BEAUTIFUL

'FINALE' FROM CABARET FRED EBB/JOHN KANDER

On 1 December 1971 the financial press announced that Biba had secured a deal to move to the other side of Kensington High Street, into the premises then occupied by the Derry & Toms department store. The building, which was twenty times the size of the current shop, was to be bought, it was reported, under a joint venture by Dorothy Perkins and British Land – the first mention of the company that was ultimately to prove Biba's downfall. For now, however, Fitz was in a bullish mood when responding to questions about the huge step they were taking: 'It sounds a big jump, but funnily enough it isn't. Our sales are already enough to put us over break-even at Derry & Toms, and the real point is that we've got 100,000 a week store-traffic at Biba now, with too little space to display the right quality of merchandise … It's the ultimate.' Despite appearances, he insisted, 'Of all the moves we have made, this is undoubtedly the safest.'

The building was one that Barbara had long coveted. Press stories that even pre-Biba she 'used to go past it, patting it and vowing that one day it would be hers' are almost certainly far fetched, but her interest in the property did at least go back to the latter days of the Church Street shop, when she passed it as she walked round the corner to the Cyril Lord store: 'It was so beautiful and so unappreciated. No one there had any respect for the building or its superb detail.' Her task, as she saw it, was to 'bring it back to its original splendour'.

Derry & Toms was one of the longest established of shops in Kensington, its roots dating back to the Toms family grocery, founded in the 1820s. In the middle of the century Christiana Toms married a local draper, Charles Derry, and the arrival of the tube network brought the two firms together in premises at 107–111 Kensington High Street, with the beginnings of a department store. A series of expansions resulted by 1900 in a property that extended from number 99, on the corner of King Street (now Derry Street), all the way up to 119. The First World War, however, hit profits so badly that in 1920 the company sold out to its bigger and more powerful neighbour, John Barker & Company. By the 1930s, therefore, when the current building was erected, Derry & Toms was actually a branch, albeit unacknowledged, of Barker's. (The third major department store in Kensington, Pontings, was also swallowed up by Barker's.)

The chief architect for Barker's at the time was Bernard George, who worked for the company between 1928 and 1962, and who indeed never had

RIGHT: *The exotics counter on the ground floor of Big Biba, designed by Whitmore-Thomas.*

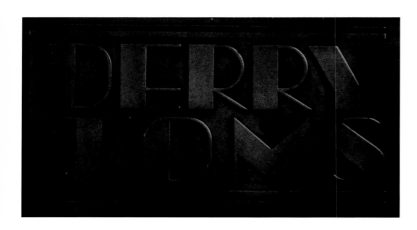

another professional position. His two great works were the twin buildings on the south side of Kensington High Street, separated by Derry Street: on the one side, the Barker's store, on the other Derry & Toms. Of the two, it is the latter, constructed in 1933, that has been the more critically unappreciated. 'A large dull rectangle,' sniffs one guide to London architecture, while even at the time it was not exactly trumpeted: it 'seems to be quite modern in its own peculiar way,' reported *Building* magazine, 'but upon closer examination it may be seen to have borrowed a good deal from the past, even if that past is no further back than the Paris Exhibition of Decorative Art.'

In fact there is much that is good about the building. The plan may indeed be an unremarkable rectangle, but the decoration was always carefully considered: the impressive high-level Portland stone reliefs depicting scenes of labour and technology were by C. J. Mabey, while the cast-iron grilles representing the signs of the zodiac were designed by Walter Gilbert, who had earlier been responsible

for the gates at Buckingham Palace. And once inside the store, the lifts, adorned by bronze panels also by Gilbert, took one to the fifth-floor Rainbow Room, a triumphant piece of modernism: 'This is one of the best examples of indirect lighting we have seen,' enthused the architectural press, 'the ceiling seems to float overhead as though one were inside a balloon … Red, green and blue tubes in each slot allow a pleasant diversity of colourings to be rendered.' It was, said the *New Yorker*, 'in a class with such masterpieces as the Chrysler Building and Radio City Music Hall.' Atop it all was the Roof Garden, designed by Ralph Hancock, that opened in 1938, and which offered some of the best views of London, as well as a haven of peace away from the crowds and the traffic of Kensington.

In 1957 Barker's was bought by the House of Fraser and, although it was to take fifteen years to resolve, the absurdity of owning two adjoining stores, theoretically in competition with each other, was always considered a problem by the new owners. When it was finally decided to off-load Derry & Toms, there was no shortage of interest: 'Do you realise,' asked Fitz at the time, unaware of the irony that history was to bestow upon his words, 'we were bidding against Marks & Spencer, British Home Stores, the lot?' In the event, he claimed, it was Sir Hugh Fraser himself 'who turned the tide for us: he has a soft spot for Derry's thirties décor and knew we would keep it that way' – though the financial success of Biba and, particularly, its backing from Dorothy Perkins and British Land were presumably also contributory factors in the sale.

'By the time it closed its doors,' noted the *New Yorker*, 'Derry & Toms was reduced to sorely faded glory. Dowdy merchandise, largely ignored by saleswomen and customers alike, lay jumbled around.' In fact, as a Kensington resident of the time recalls, 'The only thing that was amazing was the Roof Garden, which was fantastic. They had a tearoom up there, a very old-fashioned tearoom with chrome jugs, the sort of thing I can remember from when I was taken shopping by my auntie when I was nine or ten.' Others too find their memory of Derry & Toms dominated by the tearoom; Angie Bowie, later to become a regular

visitor at Biba, insists that it served 'the best high tea on Kensington High Street'. Despite this attraction, the store was locked in a time-warp, resembling nothing so much as Grace Brothers, the fictional setting for the sitcom *Are You Being Served?* (first broadcast in September 1972). Even when *Vogue* ran a puff-piece, it was hard to avoid bathos: 'Derry & Toms is best known for its roof gardens, duck ponds and woods far above the traffic. Take children there and to tea in the Rainbow Room. Take yourself to see the Polly Peck clothes, the Susan Small collection, and the best ribbon collection of any store in London.'

One of the 24 room sets in
the household department on
the fourth floor of Big Biba.
The displays were intended to
show how even an Earl's
Court bedsit could be cheaply

transformed using Biba paint,
wallpaper (supplied in
poster-sizes of 20 x 30 inches)
and fittings.

Derry & Toms was, in short, doomed, but it was to struggle on for a further eighteen months, while Biba wound itself up for the 'big jump', and Barbara prepared for what *The Sunday Times* called 'the greatest gamble of her career'.

———

The challenge was primarily the sheer scale of the operation. The existing Biba, in the old Cyril Lord premises, was already seen as a department store, but the move to Derry & Toms was bound to produce a complete transformation. Hitherto everything that hadn't actually been designed by Barbara (the jewellery from Adrian Mann and by Butler & Wilson, the hats by Molly Parkin and so on) had at least been personally approved by her, and the question arose: Was it feasible to continue this practice when there were seven storeys to fill? And the answer from Barbara was: Yes. In fact, it was the only way that it was going to happen. Biba had been, from the outset, her creation, and she wasn't going to give it up now on the very verge of achieving her dream.

Whitmore-Thomas, by now the designers of choice at Biba, were offered the chance to work on some of the new store, but held out for the whole contract, which they won, in a move seemingly calculated to make the gamble even greater. The two partners were then no more than 30 years old and this was unquestionably the biggest commission they had undertaken, covering not merely the interiors but also the graphics, packaging and advertising for the entire project. They moved their

drawing-boards out from Steve Thomas' bedroom, took some studio space and recruited more staff as they began to expand the image of Biba.

Big Biba – as the Derry & Toms building was soon known – was to represent a departure in style for the company. The late-sixties Art Nouveau incarnation had provided a strong element of fantasy, but it was essentially a very straight, even serious attitude. What Whitmore-Thomas added was a feeling of fun and play, bouncing ideas off the existing perception of Biba: 'Because the brand was

YOU COULD HAVE A SENSE OF HUMOUR, YOU COULD HAVE KITSCH WITHIN THE DESIGN AND SEND YOURSELVES UP

so strong,' explains Thomas, 'you could have a sense of humour, you could have kitsch within the design and send yourselves up.'

It was an approach that fitted the shift in culture as Britain entered the seventies, a development that was epitomised by Mr Freedom. A boutique founded by Tommy Roberts, Mr Freedom had started in the old Hung On You premises in Chelsea and had recently moved to Kensington Church Street; revelling in pop art and kitsch, it dealt in spangly hot pants and dungarees and adult-size boy-scout uniforms. Unsurprisingly it was Elton John's favourite boutique. Thomas remembers taking Barbara to lunch there, with all the food coming in bright primary colours: 'She thought it was great; she was tickled pink.' Biba never followed down the route of Mr Freedom, certainly in terms of clothes, but the camp tendency was to be felt in the store's design.

Barbara's instinct was to work with people whom she respected, and then trust them. Suggestions would be made and discussions held, but essentially the members of her design team had always been

expected to develop ideas that could then be approved or, very occasionally, rejected: the latter seldom happened, since her ability to spot talent was – apart from her own design genius – perhaps her greatest strength. 'We were given a very loose outline brief,' Thomas said, 'consisting basically of the areas to be allowed for each counter on each floor, based on the predicted sales pattern.' Kasia Charko, an illustrator who joined the Whitmore-Thomas team, has similar memories: 'I used to see Barbara Hulanicki and show her my drawings. It was very intimidating but she was such a sweet person, very shy, and because she started out as an illustrator as well, she was very kind to me. It was lovely once I got into the swing of it; they trusted me to do something they liked and just left me on my own doing things, and it snowballed.'

The period between the completion of the deal on Derry & Toms and the opening was frantic even by Biba's standards, and meant that all other existing projects – from the boutique in Bergdorf Goodman through to the embryonic Biba car – were abandoned. Barbara and Fitz had always been what would later be known as workaholics (even in 1966 it was noticeable that 'they used to work like crazy, they never stopped; their life was just the shop'), and their attitude spread to the rest of the team. 'It was a seven days and seven nights a week job,' remembers Shirley Shurville. Now, with a major building conversion on their hands and a huge expansion of products to be designed, sourced and labelled, the pressure was really on: 'It meant working seven days a week, 18 hours a day, but we did it.' And key to that process was the enthusiasm inspired by Barbara's own work ethic.

'A lot of people would go in and help,' says Malcolm Bird. 'You just helped out. You just did. If you were working for someone else, you wouldn't do that, but with Barbara it was different. She would never talk down to people and go home leaving them to do it.'

The conversion of the store itself was hampered by the fact that Derry & Toms continued to occupy the building – a mere sixteen weeks was allowed for the actual work – and it was impossible to do a full, measured survey. Fortunately the structure that Bernard George had originally created, with a regular grid of columns, allowed a replica of a section of the shop floor to be re-created in the Bracknell warehouse, and the various units and fittings were built around the columns to be transported to London when the time came. More serious were the installation of escalators from ground to first floor (lit by bronze statues of women bearing lamps) and the complete re-laying of services to the basement. Meanwhile it had been decided that the ground, first and fifth floors should have marble floors; Steve Thomas has memories of stressful trips to Portugal to try to find sufficient quantities of the rock for the purpose – when supplies of the best quality marble had been exhausted, blemished stone had to be used, but was carefully marked up to be laid under the display units, so that the whole came to resemble a giant, numbered jigsaw puzzle.

Gradually the structure of the store emerged. The ground floor was 'a grand, almost Hollywood environment' that celebrated the Art-Deco nature of the building. It housed the record department, with perhaps the finest listening booths ever seen in Britain, a bookstall selling up-market art and design volumes, and a Casbah area with North African and Middle Eastern products. Also here were knitwear, tights and cosmetics, but the floor was mostly noted for the vast amount of open space it allowed.

The first storey represented 'the core of the old Biba': the women's clothes section, where the heart of Art Nouveau still beat strong. There was just one counter – selling a bewildering selection of t-shirts and jerseys – with the rest of the stock hanging on the familiar bentwood hat stands, that had started as a makeshift option back in Abingdon Road and

Part of the Egyptian-themed
changing room on the first
floor of Big Biba, with (right)
detail from the original
sketch. Designed by
Whitmore-Thomas.

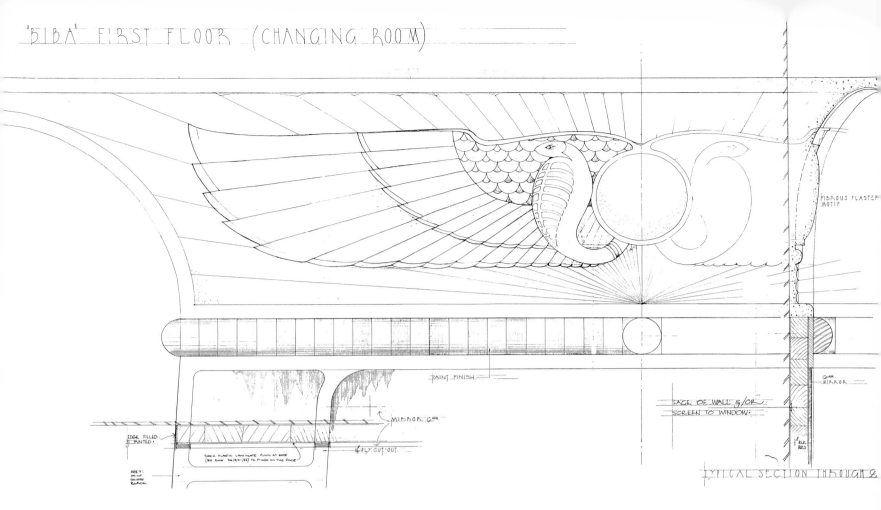

FIBROUS PLASTER MOTIF

PAINT FINISH

6mm MIRROR

FACE OF WALL &/OR SCREEN TO WINDOW.

MIDBOB. 6mm

1 BLK BRD

EDGE FILLED & PAINTED.

BLACK PLASTIC LAMINATE PLINTH AT BASE (SEE DWG No 18/01/82) TO FINISH ON THE FACE.

4 PLY CUT-OUT.

FRET: PAINT GLOSS BLACK

TYPICAL SECTION THROUGH 2

had become a symbol of the store. In the process, however, the pieces had been reclaimed from their junk status to become valuable items, as Barbara and Fitz discovered when buying for the Cyril Lord shop. 'There's a rich idiot buying up all the hat stands in London for his new shop and he'll pay anything,' they were told, and prices had risen accordingly. They resorted to having the stands made in Czechoslovakia, a necessary compromise given the quantities in which they were now required – in Kensington Church Street there had been 29 hat stands; by the time of the auction that followed the closure of Big Biba more than 200 such pieces were sold off from the first floor.

Everything was on the same grand scale: 'We'd always wanted Egyptian changing rooms,' said Steve Thomas, 'so we had Egyptian changing rooms.' It was an appropriate and timely reminder of the roots of Art Deco: the discovery of

Tutankhamen's tomb in 1922 had helped shape the style when it was first born; 50 years later the record-breaking exhibition of the tomb's treasures at the British Museum helped fuel the Deco revival, of which Biba was such a crucial part.

The second floor contained the children's department, a section for pre- and early-teen girls called Lolita, and one called Pregnant Mums for maternity wear. The latter featured extra-large shop furniture 'intended to make expectant mothers feel that they have shrunk, like Alice in Wonderland, to miniscule proportions.' But it was the children's area that was one of the great triumphs of the store, with fittings that – on Barbara's strict instructions – were essentially fun: there was a Snoopy doghouse, a giant record-player roundabout, a café with huge toadstools and a castle with a moat. All were built by FTV, a firm more normally associated with filmsets, under the direction of Tony Grasemark,

and their involvement produced a series of design questions that don't normally arise in a refurbishment project: 'What age do you want this castle?' they would ask. 'How about some dog piss down this wall?' Behind such arcane considerations was the radical idea that children might want to enjoy a shopping trip as well as their mothers, so there was also a play area, while inside the castle there would be a storyteller on Saturdays 'to keep the youngsters amused'.

Less successful was the third floor where the menswear was displayed. Always a poor relation, the established range was now joined by a section for boys between the ages of ten and fourteen that didn't quite convince: 'There are dressing gowns that Noel Coward would have considered decadent, and floppy fur coats that Lady Docker might have shunned,' reported Bevis Hiller. (It should be noted that these weren't real furs – Biba had stocked fur in 1967, but had long since turned its back on the material.) There were also 'ivory-topped canes for the dandy, and fencing masks to wear when fighting duels.' And then there was the Mistress Room, 'made to look like a lush, pink, Hollywood-style bedroom complete with mammoth bed', where a gentleman might buy the occasional piece for the unofficial lady in his life. More talked about than visited, the Mistress Room featured long satin gloves, naughty negligées, edible underwear and other pieces of ersatz erotica. All were principally bought in from outside for, despite the heady cocktail of glamour, sophistication and sensuality that Biba had made its own, it was noticeable that it never really dealt in lingerie – the whole style was built on a public allure, designed for the nightclub rather than for the bedroom.

On the fourth floor, the household and interior décor department that had begun in the previous store was allowed to run riot in a series of room-sets. Established favourites, particularly the Biba lampshades – now available in leopard-skin – were joined by a Kitch [sic] section offering, wrote Hiller, such delights as 'frilled plastic boxes, ashtrays like miniature loos, school-of-Tretchikoff paintings, nude plastic babes rising from plastic roses, urinating cupids who perform when you warm a glass bulb with your hand, and framed poems apostrophising granny.'

And then came the crowning glory of the store, the Rainbow Room on the fifth floor, originally designed as a restaurant and now returned to its former glory. The concealed lighting was restored, the fifties stage was removed to allow a reconstruction of the thirties original, recent painting was stripped away, and the installation of modern facilities (kitchen, dressing rooms, etc.) was accomplished with the minimum of disruption. So successful was the refurbishment that, despite it being the most expensive item in the entire programme, it was greeted with a response of 'Thank Christ you've kept it just as it was!' Even the *Sunday Telegraph* approved of the way it had been 'preserved intact'. 'Perhaps,' reflected Steve Thomas ruefully, 'they all "remember" it as it should have been.'

The tearooms above, on the sixth floor, were being used as a drawing-office by Whitmore-Thomas and then, after the store opened, as a studio by sculptor Andrew Logan. The one-and-a-half acres of gardens surrounding them were not to open until some six months later.

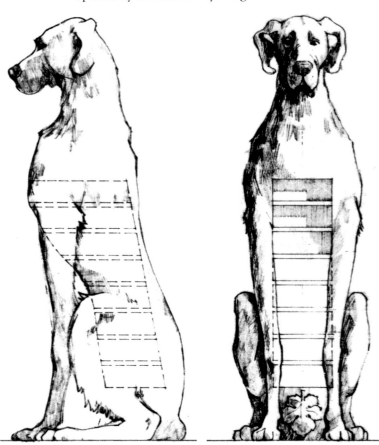

The dog-food unit in the
Food Hall basement of
Big Biba, based on Barbara's
dog, Othello, with (below)
the original sketches for
the unit. Designed by
Whitmore-Thomas.

Completing the store was the basement, which
had been converted into a food hall and represented
perhaps the finest design work of the whole project.
Here there was no Deco, no Nouveau, but instead a
witty commercial display of pop art on a grand
scale (again the FTV team were involved). Tins of
Biba baked beans were displayed within a unit
shaped like a giant baked bean tin, with cans of
soup in a similarly sized unit labelled Warhol's
Condensed, and tinned fish in a sardine can half-
opened by a massive key. Dog food was stacked

inside a scaled-up model of Barbara's Great Dane,
Othello (Steve Thomas screwed up his courage to
trace the white patch on Othello's chest in order to
make the depiction anatomically correct, whilst
taking care to add a fig-leaf), and was surrounded
by huge cat baskets filled with tinned cat food.
There was 'a skinny black skyscraper in the style of
Rennie Mackintosh to contain slimming foods like
Energen and Limmits.' Meanwhile there was a
traditional dairy, barrows for fruit and vegetables, a
mock cellar for the wine and a barge for fresh fish.

Despite the sheer joy and fun of the Food Hall, the
intention was serious. This was a foodie paradise well
in advance of its time. 'They packaged everything
with a Biba logo from baked beans to coffee, mineral
water to spices,' enthuses one habitué of the place,
'and they also had the most incredible range of
different breads.' In the Britain of the mid-seventies,
the idea of selling bottled water was almost unheard
of, while British bread was the laughing stock of
Europe – Biba was one of the first stores to make
specialist Continental bread a standard feature.

Had the full plans worked out, there would have
been even more in the basement. 'We were going to
do a fish-and-chip shop,' remembers Steve Thomas,
'and I did it as 1960s Venetian kitsch. But Barbara
said, "You've got the brick size wrong; Venetian
bricks aren't like that. Haven't you ever been to
Venice?"' He hadn't and, in pursuit of the twin
goals of perfectionism and adventurism that
characterised the Biba ethos, Barbara, Fitz, Thomas
and Eleanor Powell took off for a weekend in
Venice to check the details of an installation that,
for cost reasons, was never actually built.

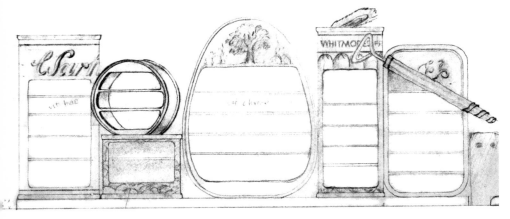

RIGHT: *Display units in the Food Hall basement at Big Biba, including Whitmore's Frankfurters and Thomas' Baked Beans, with (above) sketches of the units. Designed by Whitmore-Thomas.*

An even greater loss was the mooted movie-house on the fifth floor – 'a 150-seater cinema open all day and very late at night, showing Garbo films plus good children's films.' The proposal was for sofas grouped around coffee tables, the latter suitably placed for drinks and ashtrays, so movie-goers could relax in comfort.

Although the cinema didn't happen, the attitude it encapsulated was the dominant theme of Big Biba. This was designed to be, above all else, somewhere for people to live, not simply to shop, somewhere to be and to be seen, a private members' club for the general public. 'It is clearly intended to be a place where people can relax while they shop,' noted the *Sunday Telegraph*. 'With this end in view, darts and indoor bowls are provided in the men's department, for use either by bored male shopping companions or undecided customers.' It was claimed that 'on the ground floor alone, more seats were provided than in the public hall at Euston station.' Most significant of all were the windows. Biba simply didn't do window displays, it never had, but ever since Church Street it had provided seats in the windows for its customers who wanted to rest, weary from shopping, or who merely wished to hang out with their friends. Now,

LEFT: *One of the logos from the Food Hall at Big Biba, designed by Whitmore-Thomas.*

BELOW: *Tea caddy from Big Biba, with (right) the tea-counter in the Food Hall. Designed by Whitmore-Thomas.*

presented with 226 feet of frontage on Kensington High Street, the approach remained exactly the same. Except that there were a lot more sofas and armchairs than there had ever been before. Favourable critics hailed it as representing 'a more mature relationship between management and customer than is usual' in which both parties 'contribute more to the experience of shopping, and they expect more.' Others weren't so sure.

———

Apart from the technical and logistical challenges presented by the conversion, there was the question of stock. Uniquely, this was going to be a department store that sold almost entirely its own products: 'seven floors of retail, all own-brand throughout'. Filling the food hall inevitably meant that other manufacturers were involved – the ice cream, for example, came from the celebrated Marine Ices in Chalk Farm – but for the most part it was dressed in the familiar Biba livery. Even the wine (a fearsome English drink that was 19 per cent proof) came with a black-and-gold label, that stated not the year but the month of bottling, in a parody of traditional vintages.

Crucially, every item was authorised by Barbara herself, ensuring that it fitted her vision of how she would want to live. What had started as a tiny boutique with one dress available in one size, had within a decade become a fully fledged department store, with thousands of products bearing the official Biba stamp. And, setting a standard for brand marketing, Biba was proud to show its face

to the public; the earlier experiment with diaries and cigarette lighters was extended into every field that anyone could think of: playing cards, aftershave, crayons, luggage, colouring books, even those iconic baked beans – all bore the imprint of Biba.

Back in 1969 the *Daily Mail* had heralded the first High Street store as 'the first time that anyone in this country has been adventurous enough to try to make the British woman have the totally planned look that's seen everywhere outside these isles.' In the light of the ambitions of Big Biba, that was looking like a distant, timid approach to marketing. Now the idea was, says Steve Thomas, that 'you bought into the brand completely; this is total

involvement, total lifestyle.' And in an attempt to make sense of this cornucopia of commodities, Whitmore-Thomas created a new set of logos; the established mark designed by John McConnell was retained for the first floor, reflecting the origins of the company, but every other department now had its own logo (a total of 17) and even its own typeface, all identifiably Biba, but part of a range of images celebrating the diversity of the new store. And with them came a light-heartedness, an attitude of frivolity that played almost with self-mockery.

For some it was all too much. 'Going there is more like joining a club than patronising a store,' noted the *New York Times*. 'But the style is so uniform, and so pervasive, that "total" seems to shade into totalitarian.' For the most part, however, the previews of the Derry & Toms store were positive. No one 'could fail to be stunned by the sheer scope of the enterprise,' said the *Evening*

Standard, while *Vogue* celebrated 'a palace of apricot marble, coloured counters and fake leopardskin walls; six floors of 1930s fantasy,' and Eve Pollard in the *Sunday Mirror* proclaimed it 'the most beautiful department store in Britain.' The *Sunday Times* went further and gave it a three-page spread, saying, 'We wish her well … it is exciting to see Miss Hulanicki tackling a huge project her way – and we like humble beginnings turning into happy endings.' And, returning to where it had all started in 1964, the *Daily Mirror* offered its readers an exclusive black-and-crème crepe dress designed by Barbara Hulanicki (though it was noticeable that, although wages had nearly doubled in the intervening years, the new dress was more than eight times the price of the original gingham frock).

The positive notices reflected the attention that Biba was now paying to PR detail. Fitz made a complete circuit of Fleet Street and at every

opportunity talked up the venture as a logical extension of what Biba had been: 'It's a natural progression really. Even if we get the same number of customers that we do now, it will still be worthwhile. At the moment half of them walk out without buying anything because they can't get near the counter.' That was the critical equation: 'We will need to convert sightseers into customers,' he admitted. He also acknowledged that: 'We have consciously opened up our market and gone up the age bracket.'

But amidst the barrage of enthusiasm there were even then still, small voices raising doubts about the advisability of the endeavour. 'It must be one of the biggest gambles taken in the retail world for a long time,' cautioned the *Financial Times*. 'The whole success of this great edifice depends on the taste and flair of one person. The idea is still essentially that of the small, individually run, highly personalised boutique, but what no one knows, because it has never been tried before, is whether it can work when expanded into the proportions of a giant

department store.' Fitz shrugged off such worries, in public at least: 'I was told nine years ago that we wouldn't be here in five years' time, so I'll take a chance on still being here in another ten,' he announced, and returned to the endless round of promotion and planning.

The Derry & Toms incarnation of Biba opened on 10 September 1973. On the same day ten people accused of planting car bombs outside the Old Bailey and Scotland Yard – the first attacks by the Provisional IRA in the capital – went on trial in Winchester Crown Court; to mark the event, bombs were exploded in British Rail stations at King's Cross and Euston, with further London bombs following over the next few days. Internationally, the news that week was dominated by the military coup that overthrew the government of Chile and saw the murder of Salvador Allende; by the heightening of

LEFT: *Some of the vast range of own-brand products sold in the Food Hall at Big Biba, designed by Whitmore-Thomas.*

BELOW: *Cover of the newspaper printed to launch Big Biba, 1973.*

OVERLEAF: *Centre pages of the launch newspaper, illustrating the range of the new store.*

the conflict between Israel and Syria (13 Syrian jets were shot down over the Mediterranean) and by the continuing descent of Richard Nixon into the morass of the Watergate conspiracy.

It was a world of increasing insecurity, but Big Biba was there to offer the possibility of relief for those who wished it. Launched with the first paid advertisements it had ever taken out in the national dailies, the store was an instant success. Indeed the biggest problem was that, with so many people turning up, large numbers were unable to reach a counter to make a purchase. Determined to go home with a souvenir, the crowds descended on the Food Hall, where the paper carrier bags proved to be hugely desirable, and where the unprecedented variety of breads was the first port of call for those who just wanted to buy something, anything. 'By eleven o'clock that morning,' Shirley Shurville recalls, 'I got a phone call from Fitz saying, "They've run out of bloody bread; get down there and get some bread in".' Also popular was the Biba own-brand washing powder: the first consignment of boxes had been misprinted with the colours reversed, so that what should have been a black woman washing white clothes showed instead a white woman with black laundry – so great was the demand, however, that by the end of the week, the misprints were on the shelves in an attempt to keep the customer satisfied.

The first night of the Rainbow Room restaurant was even more chaotic. An estimated 5,000 customers were served but, despite the presence of extra staff from Grosvenor House, most had to wait two hours for their food to arrive. Again Shurville, together with Eleanor Powell, was sent in to sort out the problems: the determined efficiency of the core Biba staff remained one of the store's greatest assets. Amongst the changes they wrought, a woman from the wages office was discovered to have a particularly attractive handwriting style and was drafted in (at extra pay) to write out all the menus.

DERS. DOWN IN THE LIFTS UP THE STAIRCASES.

YOU MEET AN OLD FRIEND IN THE BAR. CELEBRATE. LOSE A TURN.

COME TO THE CABARET, OLD CHUM.. WE HAVE SOME VERY FAMOUS STARS IN THIS PARTICULAR HEAVEN.

"NICE TO SEE THE CHILDREN ENJOYING THEMSELVES ISN'T IT."

"I CAN'T HEAR YOU FOR THE SOUND OF POTATO CRISPS."

THIS IS THE RAINBOW ROOM. A BIT LIKE BEING ON THE QUEEN MARY.

BIBAS NEW PAINT COLOURS ARE SO WEIRD, YOU OFFER TO REPAINT SNOOPY'S KENNEL.

AS YOU ARE ASTOUNDINGLY RICH, YOU ORDER 365 PLACE SETTINGS OF GILT CUTLERY. YOU WON'T HAVE ANY WASHING-UP TO DO FOR A YEAR.

(THIS IS A SPECIAL ORDER, SO LOSE A TURN)

YOU DECIDE ON A NEW WALLPAPER FOR YOUR BEDROOM. COME DOWN TO THE GALLERY AND SEE HOW PRETTY IT LOOKS, HUNG.

N OLD FLAME NDS YOU OKING AT THE WELLERY IN E MISTRESS ROOM.

HAND IN HAND, YOU GO DOWN AND BUY A DOZEN LILIES OF THE VALLEY IN THE FLOWER SHOP.

9 9 9 9 9 9

YOU BREAK THE WORLD RECORD SCORE ON THE PIN-TABLES. GO TO THE RAINBOW ROOM FOR A CHAMPAGNE CELEBRATION. THE PRESS ARE WAITING.

YOU'RE PUTTING ON YOUR TOP HAT, PUTTING ON YOUR WHITE TIE, PICKING UP YOUR CANE.

YOU JUST LOOK FINE AND DANDY, SO TAKE AN EXTRA TURN.

OK VELY OLITA SS. PICK MATCH.

THANKS, PAL

DON'T YOU THINK 12 ICE CREAMS WERE A BIT TOO MUCH? YOU'LL FEEL BETTER IF YOU MISS A TURN.

YOU DO LOOK GROWN UP IN YOUR NEW CLOTHES. YOU'D BETTER GO UPSTAIRS TO THE MEN'S DEPARTMENT.

IER Y, OR CULT TER YOU

THE WEIGHT WATCHERS ARE WATCHING YOU. DO THOSE TROUSERS FEEL TIGHT? POP DOWN TO THE HEALTH FOOD COUNTER AND

THINK THIN

WELCOME TO THE GALLERY. DID YOU EVER SEE SUCH DELICIOUS UNDERWEAR BEFORE? OR NIGHTWEAR?

A FRIEND IN THE CHANGING ROOM 'BORROWS' YOUR LIPSTICK AND VANISHES. GO DOWN TO THE COSMETICS COUNTER AND BUY AN EVEN WEIRDER ONE. IT SERVES HER RIGHT.

DU'RE LOST. ASK MARY. RY SAYS YOU AN HAVE AN TRA THROW.

THE FLOWER SHOP SMELLS SO NICE. YOU MISS ONE TURN SNIFFING.

THE CASBAH: EXOTIC CLOTHES AND COSMETICS AND JEWELLERY AND RUGS AND GLASS... FROM TURKEY, TUNISIA, INDIA, MOROCCO, CHINA.

COSMETICS: A VERY NICE PLACE TO SHOW YOUR FACE... ALL THE LOVELIEST COLOURS AND THE SUBTLEST PERFUMES, AND LOTS OF KINDLY THINGS FOR SKIN.

AT NICE MAN ON E MEAT COUNTER VES YOU A BONE FOR SNOOPY. ULD YOU TAKE IT UP TO HIM, PLEASE? COND FLOOR-USE THE STAIRS.

NICE THIN FOOD

OTHELLO LIKES YOU. THROW THE DICE AGAIN.

YOU'VE GOT ALL THE FOOD FOR YOUR PARTY. BUT SOME INCENSE WOULD BE FUN. COME WITH ME TO THE CASBAH...

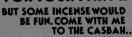

LEFT: *The Rainbow Room – 'a bit like being on the Queen Mary'.*

RIGHT: *Unused ticket for the first New York Dolls concert, 1973.*

The selection of food was, by the standards of the time, relatively adventurous, combining cosmopolitan tastes with traditional English fare. A typical menu from 1974 shows starters that included biriani with yoghurt (55p), Italian pie (30p) and Spanish frittata (30p); main courses such as roast beef with three vegetables (£1.20), ham with pease pudding and two vegetables (£1.10) and egg, bacon, sausage, tomato and fried bread (86p); and a range of desserts that featured syllabub (40p) and pouff's pudding (25p). A carafe of house wine came in at £1.50 a litre, while a litre of Bollinger was £7.50. 'It is not a place to go if you are broke or in a hurry,' wrote Mirabel Cecil, 'but great fun and relaxing, with excellent food.' She also noted the irony that Biba's revivalism had, in this venerable building, found the perfect home for its cutting edge fashion: 'The old Derry & Toms clientele with their authentic cloches and cardigans mingle with the new customers in similar clothes bought new downstairs.'

The Rainbow Room was always intended as the showpiece of the store. Open until two o'clock in the morning (except for Sundays, when it closed at midnight), it aimed to draw a partying crowd that would enhance Biba's chic status. And crucial to that was the idea that the place could become a venue for concerts. The first gig came a month after opening when Procol Harum played on 15 October 1973, a performance that was filmed for broadcast in the USA on *Midnite Special*.

The key event, however, was the two-night stint by the New York Dolls on 26 and 27 October. The Dolls had already visited Britain the previous year,

when they had supported Rod Stewart at Wembley and suffered the death of their drummer, Billy Murcia, but the Biba gigs came at a particularly critical time. Their first album, adorned with a cross-dressing cover shot (they looked 'like a gang of murderous queens'), had just been released, and in London they found themselves hailed as conquering heroes: everyone from Paul McCartney to Malcolm McLaren turned out to see them light the touchpaper of the British punk movement. 'All these people got dressed up and came and made a thing of it,' recalled singer David Johansen. 'It was like: We've got this costume, where are we gonna go in it?'

On paper, it seemed like a terrible mismatch between the cool, studied glamour of Biba and the drink- and drug-fuelled rock & roll circus of the Dolls, however much they protested otherwise. ('Why are you playing Biba?' a journalist asked, and Johansen replied: 'Because we like playing a cabaretish situation.') In reality, however, it was even messier than anyone could have anticipated.

'They ripped us off bow-legged,' exclaims Shirley Shurville. 'They went through the floors taking stuff.' And certainly it's true that bassist Arthur 'Killer' Kane was arrested even before the first gig by store detectives, but the defence was solid: 'Arthur tried on a black jacket with a leopard collar which was priced at £40. We didn't have any money, so Arthur switched the price tag on it for a £12 one. He wasn't shoplifting…'

The gigs themselves were no less anarchic. Ian Dickson, who photographed the concert, remembers that the attitude of pilfering had spread to the entire rock industry on the nights, with music-biz people helping themselves to whatever they could lay their hands on. Meanwhile the band had a rider that included 40 bottles of champagne, and the five of them appeared to have taken full advantage of the facilities: 'They were all drunk,' says Kasia Charko, 'well, I don't know who was more drunk, us or them. They were amazing, just funny. It was really strange: the Rainbow Room was quite sedate, but they were on something.' The fact that both guitarist Johnny Thunders and drummer Jerry Nolan were fast acquiring a fondness for heroin did nothing to stabilise the performance. 'They were perfect,' remembers photographer Mick Rock, whilst the future Adam Ant was another one of many blown away by the event: 'They were amazing.'

For Biba, whatever was originally intended, the booking was seen as a very definite declaration of intent: 'It was a very hip statement,' says Mick Rock. 'The Dolls were operating under the radar, in that they were probably not a nationally known band, though they were certainly known in the community.' At a time when the biggest British rock star was David Bowie, and when his legions of fans were following his advice to look to the New York underground of Max's Kansas City, the New York Dolls were seen as part of the art-glam world that also embraced the likes of Lou Reed and Iggy Pop. For them to have appeared at Biba so early on in its new venue sealed its reputation as 'the glam party centre' or, as the *Melody Maker* put it, 'the hallowed Mecca of the near-decadent.'

Subsequent gigs lacked the wildness of the Dolls, with appearances by, amongst others, the Troggs, Bill Haley & His Comets, George Melly, Manhattan Transfer, the Pointer Sisters, Ten Years After, the Ronettes and Kilburn & The High Roads. But even the most innocuous-sounding booking could disrupt the poise of the store: a two-night appearance by Screaming Lord Sutch saw the second evening fall apart when a member of the audience provoked His Lordship into a fist fight.

The setting of 'the outrageously camp Rainbow Room' was enhanced by the routine of having a full three-course dinner served to musicians and audience alike before the concert. For fans of a group like the Average White Band, more used to seeing them perform in clubs and colleges, it could be a disconcerting experience: 'It was very stilted in a way, because there was no waiting for something to happen – you could see the group. It was the sort of place you'd go to eat and listen to some background music.' Another at the same gig, however, found the democracy of the dinner appealing: 'It took away the untouchable aspect of it all, and I personally liked that.' There was also

the unique slant that Biba brought to the billing; Cockney Rebel played a publicity showcase there in January 1974, when they were one of the hottest cult acts in the country, and found themselves supported by the veteran dance-band leader Blanche Coleman and her all-girl band, plus a mime troupe.

Most spectacular of all was the appearance of Liberace at a private banquet for members of his British fan club. 'He adored the store,' reported Barbara, surprising no one, 'particularly the leopard skin luggage.' Steve Thomas designed a cake for the occasion, in – naturally – the shape of a four-foot long grand piano.

The space next to the Rainbow Room was where the cinema had been planned; when that idea fell through, it was turned into an exhibition and gallery area, used particularly for the launch of two major books: Norman Mailer's *Marilyn Monroe*, and *Rock Dreams*, a collaboration between writer Nik Cohn and Belgian artist, Guy Peellaert. The latter, with its realist depictions of rock stars in fantasy situations, brought out the celebrities. 'Angie and I had both seen the book,' wrote David Bowie in his diary column in *Mirabelle*, 'and when we learned that the drawings were to be displayed at Biba in London, we decided that we just had to get along and look at them. Biba ... has an up-to-the-minute appearance combined with a lovely, nostalgic feel of the thirties. The building is enormous, and quite palatial, in fact it is really grand and the paintings had attracted an enormous crowd.' Whilst there, Bowie met Peellaert and a commission for the cover of his next album, *Diamond Dogs*, followed.

Angie Bowie herself became for many Bibaphiles almost the epitome of the Derry & Toms years, with her androgynous, assertive image capturing and setting the mood of the times. 'I loved the store,' she says, 'I loved being in the store.' Although she admits she took care when passing through to the Rainbow Room or Roof Garden: 'I used to carry my purse in front of me and not touch anything, because I knew they had a problem with shoplifters and I didn't want them to think I was one.'

The timing was perfect. The all-embracing hedonism of Big Biba coincided with the rise of glam, as ex-mods David Bowie, Marc Bolan and Bryan Ferry dragged British rock into a camp celebration of play, while round the corner in Chelsea *The Rocky Horror Show* was dressing musicals up to the nines. And Biba was by now the biggest dressing-up box in the country. Lou Reed wore the black nail polish, as

*One of the speakers for
the in-house sound system
at Big Biba, designed by
Whitmore-Thomas.*

did Freddie Mercury, whose girlfriend, Mary Austin, worked at Biba, and who supported the store right through to the end. 'It's really a beautiful shop done up well,' he enthused in 1975. 'When fans come over here, that ought to be the first place they go.' There was even a drag queen undergoing hormone treatment who renamed herself Biba.

Like the gigs, the parties too played a major role in the appeal: 'It was a constant event,' remembers Mick Rock. Particularly lavish was the launch for the Roof Garden in spring 1974, that came complete with fire-eaters, tightrope-walkers and a string quartet. 'That was a wild affair,' says Rock, 'it must have cost them a bundle. I suppose there was a sort of promotion that went on with it, but I think they

just did it to do it, because they wanted to do it, because they liked it.' The Roof Garden was now home to a menagerie of birds – ducks, doves, flamingos and penguins were brought in (though the penguins failed to settle and eventually had to be returned) – as well as a series of 15-foot-high flowers constructed by sculptor Andrew Logan and installed in the Tudor Garden. The place became the cherished haunt of many: 'The Roof Garden was where you just were; you floated around and looked divinely decadent. You looked out through those lovely Deco roundels down Kensington High Street and just wandered about, looking at everyone else.'

'Walk into the new Biba,' said the *Evening News*, 'and you'll feel as if you've stepped inside a dream machine.' It was an impression that many were to share: 'It was like a strange Disneyland', 'like walking into Narnia', 'like stepping in off the cold reality of the street into fairyland.' *The New Yorker* acclaimed it as being 'what a department store should be … a unique synthesis of promenade, living theatre, movie palace, gallery and classroom of taste as well as marketplace.'

What Biba offered, reflects Steve Thomas, was 'fantasy for the night: you can be Garbo, you can be Marilyn. It took girls out from being second-class citizens, secretaries and shop girls, to being stars, because boys fell apart at the sight of them. Blokes' jaws dropped when Biba girls went out on the town. It was an important transference of image.' That Pygmalion effect had long been the stock in trade of

Biba, but Derry & Toms went further by offering a setting worthy of such a transformation. 'The lifts, when they were working, were superb,' says one enthusiast. 'And the stairwell was magnificent; if you could get to walk down it with nobody else around, you felt like a million dollars.' Marco Pirroni remembers going up the escalator and hearing for the first time Roxy Music's new single 'Street Life' on the in-house sound system; as close to glam heaven as one could get.

The worsening economic situation in the world generally, and in Britain in particular, was ensuring that popular culture's fondness for the past was unlikely to diminish. Artists like the Pasadena Roof Orchestra, Manhattan Transfer and Bette Middler went back beyond rock & roll for their influences, while music from Busby Berkeley movies and the Swing Era was being reissued in a process that culminated in the Glen Miller revival of 1975. And, following on from *Bonnie and Clyde*, there was a string of movies rooted in the twenties and thirties: *The Boyfriend, Cabaret, The Great Gatsby*. (Barbara was invited to design the costumes, and Whitmore-Thomas the sets for the latter film, but the preparations for Big Biba left no time for the project.)

In the most difficult period for Britain since the war, people were increasingly seeking escapism, and were turning to the same source that had sustained their parents during the Great Depression: Hollywood glamour. Big Biba's triumph was not merely to draw on that but to recreate it, building an environment that was 'more like a Busby Berkeley film set than a department store'; here you could not merely witness but participate in the fantasy.

Retailing experts, like Alistair Best in *Design* magazine, worried about the under-utilisation of space. 'Shopping is almost a fringe activity,' he wrote, adding that the venture was 'a suicidal gamble'. But for others, this was precisely what made them fall in love with the store. The sheer scale of it all meant that this was a place to spend your time rather than your money, and the more time the better. 'You'd go to the Rainbow Room,' remembers one, 'get an ice cream sundae and make it last for two hours. On Saturday you'd get dressed up to go to Biba, you'd spend all day there.' A particular

MORE LIKE A BUSBY BERKELEY SET THAN A DEPARTMENT STORE

favourite of many were the window seats, which came complete with ashtrays for those with a taste for tobacco and other related substances: 'I just liked sitting in the window, watching people going up and down outside and watching people in the shop, watching what people were wearing.'

People-watching was always a joy. 'As well as the overwhelming theatricality and glamour of it all,' recalls journalist Maggie Alderson, 'my over-riding memory is of being surrounded by beautiful people.' For young girls especially, this was the dominant impression: 'It was slightly dangerous, grown up, full of girls who actually had boyfriends and wore lipstick,' remembers one. 'Everybody was very thin,' agrees another. 'I'd never seen so many people wearing such fashionable clothes, all in one place.'

The sixties revolution of shopping as leisure was elevated beyond all measure. In addition to the droves of foreign tourists, Big Biba attracted day-trippers from outside London. 'We'd get off the train, go straight down the tube and come out into Biba, and there was this amazing world. We all came home on the five o'clock train, and we might only have a lipstick or a blusher or a peacock feather, because that's all we could afford, just a little something to say that we'd been there.' Future designer Peter Westcott was 15 years old and living in Somerset when he bunked off a school trip and 'spent the whole day at Biba, just being blown away by the sales assistants in dark green knits and the leopard-skin lampshades and the dark corners. I bought a fifteen-foot long scarf in navy and cream to wear into school, and some gold, sparkly Wellington boots – I wore them on the farm. No wonder my brother was so angry…'

'Towards the end of the day,' recalls one aficionado, 'we'd go down into the basement, buying foodstuffs, which were terribly expensive, and fresh vegetables, which were disgraceful: I'll never forget the first cauliflower I bought there – it was full of crawling things. So, having spent the week's food allowance at Biba, you then subsisted on baked beans for a week. No wonder we were all so thin!'

Even for the shop assistants it was a special experience. The expansion into Derry & Toms had brought in hundreds of new staff, even more for Saturday jobs, and the Biba appeal was still working its magic: 'I was working in a bank in the City as a secretary, and I was earning a lot more money, but I just had to go and work at Biba. I loved it, it was absolutely brilliant. I had to move back home so I was commuting two hours one-way to get to work, but I just had to do it.' Meanwhile a 16-year-old, having trouble finding work because she lived in a children's home ('people thought I was some kind of criminal'), was happily welcomed into the fold. 'I didn't feel awkward or that it was above me and, considering my age, I should have been perhaps a little more apprehensive, but I didn't feel that ever. It was a fantastic place to walk into, and you could feel comfortable there.' It was a common experience, regardless of background: 'I was totally mind-blown by the whole atmosphere of the place. And of course there were the clothes. I came from Australia, and if you had a Twiggy-type figure – which I did – you couldn't buy anything that was made for you. But Biba did such small sizes. And working there you got a 30-per-cent discount.'

'It wasn't like working,' a Saturday girl recalls. 'That's probably why the staff were so laid back; just being here was enough.' For customers this wasn't always a plus point: 'It was actually quite difficult to buy stuff, because they couldn't be bothered, they really couldn't be bothered; they'd just sit there looking amazing with green hair and green lipstick and green fingernails.' Others saw this lack of involvement as part of the charm of the shop: 'If you did want to buy anything, it took you half an hour to attract anybody's attention. I think that was one of the joys. It was wonderful: how could anyone be employed doing that? Thinking of how we had to rush around at work to get things done! Even then, everything was much faster outside, but you stopped as though you were in a time-lapse.' The relaxed attitude of the assistant

was part of the sense of separation from real life, an element in the make-believe world of Biba.

But this exotic wonderland was, reported the *Guardian*, 'a far cry from the cheap but original dolly-bird fashion concept which Barbara Hulanicki's boutique once was.' So how much had it changed? Certainly the prices, though still not on couture levels, had drifted upwards by the standards of Biba's competitors: in 1974 a pair of snakeskin shoes would cost you £13.70, whilst a similar pair were on sale for £12.99 at SAMM. And the new environment was difficult for many of those who had frequented Biba in the old days, the transformation from the over-crowded thrift-shop atmosphere proving too much: 'The size and the space just didn't suit it,' remembers one. 'Whereas all the satin and the velvet and the colours, when it was all dark and cosy, had this sort of secret boudoir feeling, suddenly it was all too big and too much.' There was a loss of exclusivity, as George Melly points out in relation to the earlier shops – 'Although it wasn't a secret, it was meant to be one' – but the scale of Derry & Toms meant that it was very definitely no longer an elite of those in the

know. Perhaps more worryingly for Biba on a long-term basis was that its association with youth was starting to tell, as the original customers got older: 'My Biba days were very much the early ones,' says a veteran of the sixties shops. 'Although you could get away with wearing Biba things when you were getting older, it was still in my mind very much a young phase.'

Even amongst those arriving for the first time, there were some who couldn't see the point. 'Everything looks like an imitation of something,' an American ballet dancer was reported as saying. 'It's like a theatrical set with nobody to watch the performance.' Which, of course, was the appeal to those who bought into the fantasy; the blurring of the roles of spectator and performer was what Biba did best. 'It was our introduction to the surreal,' says one woman who was a schoolgirl at the time. 'It was the pointlessly beautiful, the non-utilitarian sexiness of it, and the acres of space and display and the dark corners and strange colours where anything could happen.'

And then it ended.

TUMBLING DOWN

GEE, BUT IT'S HARD WHEN ONE LOWERS ONE'S GUARD TO THE VULTURES

COCKNEY REBEL: 'TUMBLING DOWN' STEVE HARLEY

In 1971 British Land and Dorothy Perkins had formed a joint company to develop retail sites, and the primary target had been the Derry & Toms building. In the event, that property was bought by British Land alone for £3.9 million, with the agreement that Dorothy Perkins would take up the lease and then sublet the premises to their subsidiary, Biba Ltd. It was a more complicated arrangement than Biba had previously known, but it was still relatively straightforward. Then, in August 1973, just one month before the store was due to open, British Land bought Dorothy Perkins – with the support of that company's directors – and became by extension the new owner of Biba.

Fitz was said to have responded to the news with a terse comment: 'That's the end of us.' Barbara later expanded on this, but the position remained much the same: 'We were just very unlucky to get stuck with awful people who were not our choice, but the result of a takeover from the people we had chosen.'

In fact the position was even more difficult. The Dorothy Perkins management with whom Biba had originally done its deal had been controlled by the Farmer family, Alan and Ian, who were 'so helpful, they really believed in Biba'. But now there was a Group Managing Director, David Roxburgh, who appeared to have little fondness for the idealism of Barbara and Fitz. By the time Big Biba opened,

therefore, it could no longer count on the total support of its immediate management, and was ultimately owned by a company whose concerns were with property not retail, a fact which British Land are happy to acknowledge: 'We were interested in real estate, not management.'

In the first months, trading was so successful that these structural problems were of little consequence. Even its detractors conceded the store was attracting 'a million visitors a week', and Roxburgh was amongst the first to celebrate the first seven days' takings. 'This week has been simply tremendous,' he was quoted as saying. 'The cash registers didn't stop ringing.' Despite the early indicators of success, however, the odds were stacked against the venture. Barbara had once reflected on the beginnings of Biba that: 'We couldn't have started at a better time – everything was going our way.' Now the opposite was the case: Big Biba opened at possibly the worst moment in post-war Britain, just as the economy started to slide completely out of control.

In 1973 both unemployment and interest rates were nearly double the levels they had been when Abingdon Road opened, and the very week of the Derry & Toms launch saw mortgage rates hit a record

RIGHT: *Hat stand display units on the first floor of Big Biba.*

high of 11 per cent. These underlying economic weaknesses were fully exposed when the Yom Kippur War broke out in October, and OPEC began to squeeze the West in support of the Palestinian people: oil imports to Britain fell by 15 per cent on the previous year, and in November the world price of oil quadrupled. Simultaneously the National Union of Mineworkers began an overtime ban, and the spectre was raised of another winter of power cuts (there had been a miners' strike in early 1972).

It turned out much worse than that. Ted Heath's government responded to the diminishing fuel supplies by imposing a three-day working week on British industry, combined with a series of other austerity measures: TV broadcasts closed down at 10.30 p.m, a speed limit of 50 m.p.h. was introduced on motorways and a state of emergency was imposed. The three-day week started on 2 January 1974 and ran through until 8 March. In the interim the miners had come out on strike, and Heath had been replaced by Harold Wilson, with little effect on the nation's decline: 1974 set post-war records for retail price inflation (up 19 per cent),

wage rates (up 29 per cent) and industrial production (down 3 per cent).

The chaos of the economy had little immediate impact on Biba's operation; emergency lighting was introduced to cope with power cuts, making the store even darker than normal, while up at the offices working conditions were far from ideal: 'We used to sit there with rugs piled on us and mittens on, and we had a miner's lamp on the desk.' But these things were tolerated. Just as significant, though less spectacular, was the decision by the Education Secretary, Margaret Thatcher, to increase the school-leaving age from fifteen to sixteen, a change implemented in September 1973: at a stroke, a year's worth of potential employees were taken out of the market, while many customers were excluded from the workforce for another twelve months, their income still reliant on pocket money rather than a wage packet.

If Biba wasn't overly affected, however, the 1974 crisis had a devastating impact on British Land.

The chairman and managing director of the company, the man who was, with David Roxburgh, to play a key role in the last phase of Biba, was John Ritblat. Just two years older than Barbara, he had set up an estate agency at the end of the fifties and by 1973 had found himself at the helm of 'one of Britain's fastest growing property companies' with a personal stake valued at £1.75 million (he'd become a millionaire by the age of 33). He was described as a man 'who eschews neither risk nor controversy', an approach that proved an asset in the long term, but in the climate of the mid-seventies left British Land potentially vulnerable; as early as 1973 analysts were pointing out that 'if market values fall, or alternatively are pegged at historically low levels, there could be severe financial problems.' A year or so later and those problems had materialised. The property slump that followed hard on the heels of the recession left British Land in a position of being 'heavily supported by its bankers'. With interest rates soaring, the share price went into freefall, collapsing from a 1974 high of 122p to just 12p by mid-September amidst 'rumours that British Land would be finding difficulty in making its quarterly interest payments.'

It was against this background, and with further rumours about the sale of Derry & Toms, that in July 1974 Barbara and Fitz drafted a press release announcing that there was 'a fundamental disagreement' between them and Dorothy Perkins over 'the further development of the Biba store'. The statement wasn't officially issued, but the disagreement remained, and in October David Roxburgh wrote to Fitz and Barbara in unequivocal terms: 'The present situation is totally unacceptable to us and to British Land and current losses must be attacked immediately … British Land have made it abundantly clear that they will have absolutely no compunction in closing down the business totally unless there is a marked improvement in the income being earned.' While acknowledging that the company was 'potentially profitable', he went on to lay down the conditions under which it would now function: 'Both of you will cease to be involved in the day-to-day management of the store and of the cosmetics business … As Chairman, I shall take on full executive responsibility for the management of the business, for policy making and for all executive implementation and action.'

THE PRESENT SITUATION IS TOTALLY UNACCEPTABLE TO US AND TO BRITISH LAND

The letter enclosed a memo to be signed by Fitz and distributed to the staff, approving the emasculation. Fitz refused to do so, but did write a letter that concluded: 'With great regret for the past Barbara and I feel we have no real alternative but to go, rather than to stay on terms which would be of real benefit to no one. It seems in the circumstances that we shall be entitled to compensation in respect of our loss of employment and you may expect to hear from our solicitors in due course.' The resignation letter was never sent, presumably

 THE BIBA STORY

Biba Cosmetics poster.
Photography: Sarah Moon;
model: Ingrid Boulting.

because sufficient grounds for constructive dismissal didn't exist, and Fitz instead pursued the possibility of a management buy-out that would liberate Biba from its parent company. His chosen partner was Mitsubishi, already working with Biba Cosmetics in Japan, but the negotiations failed.

And so began a death of a thousand cuts. By March 1975, with the Rainbow Room already reduced to being open only two nights a week, and with the closure of the third and fourth floors (menswear and household), it was clear that the battle was lost. 'This is a temporary closure,' claimed a spokesperson. 'Our closures are a result of a general bad economic situation and not an omen of Biba failing. It is difficult for us to progress when people keep spreading these rumours.' *The Times*' correspondent also made mention of the whispering campaign, talking of 'months of demoralising gossip, publicity about staff militancy, and, I suspect, a programme of calculated diminishment of Barbara's confidence.'

The managers brought in by Dorothy Perkins to run the store in place of Barbara and Fitz were trying to impose normal retailing standards on a model that was created to be wilfully abnormal. 'It was a nightmare,' says Daphne Bewes. 'We had personnel managers, and it was a nightmare. It was how we never worked; we didn't understand it and they didn't understand us.' Shirley Shurville was another still in there fighting: 'Dorothy Perkins launched themselves on us – we had them all around us, all day long. God, it was murder. Dump-bins began to appear.' More than anything else, it was this dump-bin mentality that signalled the end of Biba. 'The

whole atmosphere changed,' remembers one shop assistant, 'its soul died. They started bringing in fluorescent lights and wire racks and so on, making it just like any other shop and that's when I left.' The Biba ethos itself came under attack: 'Everywhere in the store the principle was adopted of giving less: paper cartons, not black china cups in the Rainbow Restaurant, piped music threatened instead of rock music over the loudspeakers.' Even the fabulous pop-art display units in the food hall were removed to make way for standard units (which, it was reported, 'proved to hold no more goods than the baked bean tins had done').

Emblematic of the ideological clash were the windows. To any orthodox business mind, the abuse of the space was unbelievable: instead of selling merchandise, it was simply providing a home for tramps, attracting 'all the bums in London', according to John Ritblat. To those who cared, however, these weren't any old bums, they were Biba bums. 'There was an old tramp who used to drape himself in the window,' remembers Shirley Shurville of one man who they'd known since the Cyril Lord days, 'and Dorothy Perkins came along and wanted him out. Barbara said, "Don't you dare!" because he was allowed. They couldn't understand why we didn't have window displays and why we had seats in the windows.'

Rendered impotent by, in Fitz's phrase, this 'army of little grey men', Barbara withdrew from the store. There were occasional forays – such as the time she showed up with a friend in full Arab dress, and carefully showed him round every corner of the shop, just to scare the life out of the Dorothy Perkins management with visions of a buy-out – but eventually even these ceased, and for the last few months she was effectively shut out from the business she had created.

Finally, in July 1975, British Land announced that it had secured a deal for Marks & Spencer to take a quarter of the building, including half the ground floor. John Ritblat, it was reported, marked the occasion by lighting 'a larger cigar than usual'.

At this stage there were still plans for Biba to continue trading in reduced circumstances upstairs in the Derry & Toms building, but there was little chance that Barbara and Fitz were going to agree to such a humiliation, particularly when it was made public in the patronising terms used by one of the British Land directors: 'I wouldn't say they're happy about the affair, but then I wouldn't expect them to be. We're dealing with artistic people. What remains will be enough to satisfy anyone's ego and vanity. We've all got to cut back our ambitions to the cloth we can tailor.'

And so the formal death notice was served, and on 19 September 1975 Biba shut its doors for the last time.

———————

What brought about the end of Biba? Fitz was quite clear: 'Biba was perfectly successful until interference came from the management, because the old Dorothy Perkins family were replaced by managers who suddenly found themselves king of

the castle. Then British Land's shares dropped and everyone got terribly egotistical and fuhrer-ish.'

The most commonly voiced alternative view is that Biba over-reached itself by trying to be all things to some women. They had 'bitten off more than they could chew', in the words of John Ritblat. 'They couldn't stock the store and they couldn't run it.' Even many of those more sympathetic to Barbara's philosophy tend towards the same opinion. And certainly there were huge logistical problems in stocking a store on this scale. Biba was, for example, determined to break the dull presentation of white goods, but found that specialist supplies of brown enamel cookers and black fridges were hard to come by. (There is a story that Barbara once sent back the shop's computer to IBM, saying that the standard grey box was too unattractive and demanding that it be painted purple – presumably to match the purple telephones already installed in the office.)

But this was a new store and what it primarily needed was money and time, neither of which British Land was able, or possibly inclined, to offer. More importantly, the 22-month gestation period of Big Biba had perhaps seen Barbara over-reaching on a personal level. The pressures of finally realising the ambition to have her own department store had drained even her phenomenal strength and willpower. 'To me the dream was over on September 10, 1973,' she admitted later. 'It was the doing up of the new store that was the excitement. After that it was suddenly like having ten children and being stuck with them for life.' In the subsequent fight to survive, the energy was lacking. And maybe such a fight was never going to be winnable: Barbara and Fitz had only a quarter-share of Biba by that stage and the Dorothy Perkins board were always capable of out-gunning them.

Others pointed to a possible fossilising of the style: 'The big mistake was that they didn't shift the image,' said fabric designer Allan Thomas. 'By 1975, I was trying to show them new prints, but they always wanted the same, the typical Biba. They should have known that nothing is for ever in fashion.' From an American perspective, there was also a dated attitude to service: 'Large signs mounted on each cash register stated "No returns, refunds or exchanges," a policy that was not as strange among conventional British retailers as it would have been in the States, but a policy that

progressive retailers such as Marks & Spencer were sharply challenging.' Then there was the perennial complaint about theft, now taken up by Biba's enemies. 'The stock was walking out the window,' says Ritblat. 'You couldn't buy anything, it was too dark.' And David Roxburgh claimed that the Biba management was 'culpably negligent' for 'a situation where "the whole world" was speculating on the sheer size of losses by theft, etc.'

The figures were certainly impressive: 'The store's pilfering rate was 12 per cent of turnover,' stated the *Evening Standard*, adding that Fitz claimed this was 'written into the budget'. If true, this is an extraordinary rate of loss, and by now it was believed that the main problem was not the customers but the employees, who then came under the scrutiny of the store detectives: 'There were plain-clothes security and they were predominantly looking at the staff,' remembers one employee. It wasn't an unjustified suspicion. When the store opened, a state-of-the-art till system was brought in from the German firm Anker, believed to comprise the first computerised cash registers in any major British store; within days, it's said, it had been cracked by the shop girls. (Though it remained a mystery how the money was being removed from the premises, despite searches of bags and pockets, until Fitz found that the nearby tobacconist stall was doing an unexpectedly roaring trade in Cuban cigars; it appeared that the cigars were disposed of and the money rolled into the metal tubes, which were then secreted about the person.)

Even so, Biba had coped with the steady drip of theft throughout its existence, and had still turned

in record profits. It may have become a bigger issue with the greater number of staff now employed, but it appears unlikely that it was terminal.

More simply it seems that Britain was no longer a congenial environment for the kind of creative entrepreneur that had revitalised sixties culture; visionaries were last decade's thing. Big Biba was certainly not given the time and investment to prove whether it could work – even within the first year the lack of faith from above was evident – but in the straitened circumstances of the period, no one was likely to give it that time. It couldn't have reached the stage it did without the involvement of a larger partner, in this case Dorothy Perkins, but by selling out a majority share-holding it ensured that it would never be in complete control of its fate. 'Biba's time is now unquestionably up,' said the *Observer* towards the end, with a touch of malevolence. 'It has been living in a fantasy world for too long; the dream had to end.'

Meanwhile British Land walked away, quietly satisfied with the profit it had made on the deal. 'It was only a minor episode,' reflects John Ritblat. 'It wasn't destabilising.'

━━━━━━━━━

Following the closing-down sale, the final scene was played out on 4 October 1975 when Bonham's auctioned off the fixtures and fittings in a sale titled 'Goodbye Ken High!' It was by all accounts a chaotic event, and the sums raised could hardly have made much of a dent in the debts: Lot #107 (One Timber 'Snoopy' Dog Kennel) went for £65, while Food Hall display units such as the baked beans tin and the frankfurter stand reached just £35 and £20 respectively. The children's castle was bought by Andrew Logan (it later formed the backdrop for an early Sex Pistols gig on Valentine's Day 1976), though his own flower sculptures didn't appear in the sale - he later discovered that they had been smashed and disposed of. Other pieces weren't actually sold at all, but were allegedly stolen: 'I knew a girl whose older brothers went and wrote in big felt-tip pen on mirrors and things: "Sold - deliver to..." And all these lorries turned up to deliver the mirrors to their house.'

The following year came a funeral oration from a surprising quarter. An episode of the Thames TV drama series *Rock Follies* saw the Little Ladies (played by Charlotte Cornwell, Julie Covington and Rula Lenska) wearing thirties dresses and singing 'Biba Nova', an elegy both to the store and to the style magazine that also closed in 1975:

> It's after four
> The stars won't wait
> She's feeling faint
> He's feeling fate
> They dream of 1968 and Biba-Nova
> We're gonna live forever
> Biba-Nova
> It's all over

The sense of loss never quite went away for Bibaphiles – 'I'm still sad about it today' – but it was tinged for a long time with a very real bitterness directed at the company that was seen to have been responsible for the demise. 'I didn't go in a Dorothy Perkins shop for twenty years,' says one. 'I absolutely refused to buy anything from them,' agrees another.

Barbara herself was shell-shocked by the closure. 'I was okay for two days and then it hit me,' she said. 'I didn't know who I was any more. Biba had been my life, my dream. And now it was gone. It

was like losing a child. I'm not exaggerating, to me it was as bad as that.' But she had always been resilient and was in no mood to lie down. Asked back in 1966 what she would do if the shop closed, she had replied without hesitation: 'Start another one.' Denied the use of the name Biba, which Dorothy Perkins was continuing to use for the cosmetics range (still highly profitable, it was now sold in more than fifteen countries), she found new premises to start again under a different name. 'It was love at first sight,' she said of the proposed new store.

Good-bye Ken High !

Sale of Art Deco, Furnishings, Fixtures, Fittings and Miscellany

To be conducted by
Messrs. Bonham & Sons, Ltd.,
Montpelier Galleries,
Knightsbridge, S.W.7.

Saturday, 4th October, 1975

at 12.00 noon

Price 50p
Admission by Catalogue Only

It wasn't to be. The deal on those premises fell through, as did a further three such proposals. Barbara was just 38 years old when Biba collapsed, and far from ready to be written off. She designed a range of t-shirts and shorts for Fiorucci, which was launched in April 1976, but by then she and Fitz had already left for a new challenge: starting up again in Brazil. Prudence Glynn of *The Times*, who had long been a supporter of Biba, mourned their departure: 'Every time one of our caucus of really original creative talents is pushed overseas, it diminishes us as a nation.'

But Biba had been such a strong brand name that it was not to be allowed to pass on quietly. The rights to the name were sold in 1977 to a consortium fronted by David Moxey – who had run Biba Cosmetics virtually from the outset – and backed by Iranian money. The following year the group set up shop in Conduit Street in the West End, enticing many of the old team back for one more effort; Shirley Shurville, Steve Thomas, Julie Hodgess, Tony Porter and others all signed on, and the gap at the heart of the operation was filled, in an imaginative if possibly risky strategy, by bringing in Barbara's younger sister Biruta, familiarly known as Biba Hulanicki. Biruta had also studied at Brighton Art College, though she had left after six months, and had later moved with her husband to the tiny Caribbean island of Dominica, where they had established a hotel and where she had run a boutique.

Despite substantial amounts of money and goodwill, the Conduit Street Biba was not a durable success and it closed in 1980 with debts reckoned to be around £1 million. At the same time, Barbara was making her own return to London retail with a shop in Holland Park Avenue, but times had changed and the truth was that the magic had been lost somewhere along the way: 'I liked the tweedy trousers, the reversible coats with raglan collars, a short corduroy coat dress and a cheap and cheerful tan leather jacket,' wrote a correspondent for *The Times*, giving every impression of damning with faint praise. A second outlet appeared the following year in Regent Street, with the emphasis on a new range, Minirock, aimed at girls between nine and sixteen. There was nothing wrong with the clothes or the shops, but none of it quite managed to inspire passion in the purchasers in the way that Biba had, and no one was entirely surprised when it failed to set the world alight. Similarly a range of Hulanicki Cosmetics came and went.

All of this was, in effect, an afterthought, a postscript to the Biba story. The real transforming moment, the event that launched the second half of Barbara's career, came in 1987 when Ron Wood of the Rolling Stones asked her to design his bar,

Biba poster.
Photography: James Wedge.

Woody's On The Beach in Miami. Suitably impressed, Chris Blackwell – the founder of Island Records – invited her to work on his growing chain of hotels in the South Beach area, from where there was no stopping her. She went on to revamp a smart clutch of world-famous luxury hotels and beach resorts and to become a hugely successful designer in another world.

Meanwhile, traces of the Biba experience have survived. For the 11 years of its existence, from corner shop to department store, it had entranced a generation of women, and its spell was such that even now it conjures up memories of a near-mythical near-history. Women who went there will never forget it, children who grew up in Biba nappies ('standard English Terry nappies, dyed in all the Biba colours: brown and yellow and peach and lavender') have had the story of this extraordinary store passed on to them, and the hundreds of young women who were – and are still being – named Biba bear testimony to its lasting impact. And in a world where the cultural tide is perhaps again turning against corporatism, the inspiration of a business built by one woman, without benefit of focus groups or market research, continues to inspire many who weren't even born when Biba died: 'Commerce seems such a bleak, person-less entity, and then you get a shop like Biba, which was all about the person, all about the individual.'

'For far too long,' Barbara had reflected during the glory years, 'English girls have had to suppress their natural instincts and hide in clothes chosen by their mothers. Now at last they are free.' That sense of freedom and of self-expression remains the lasting legacy of the Biba experience.

PARI'S STORY

Some of my most treasured early memories can be found in one of the most prestigious striptease-bars in Berlin, a bar called the Oasis that was owned by my aunt and uncle. He had acquired a plot of land shortly after the war in exchange for a pig (food was in short supply at the time), and had built himself a beautiful house, attached to which was the bar that my aunt was to be responsible for running on a day-to-day basis. By the time I knew it in the early-seventies, the Oasis had grown to become a very fashionable and glamorous nightclub, the kind of sophisticated establishment where the women were as enchanting as Josephine Baker and the men were simultaneously in awe and in love, torn between worshipping and wooing. Since both my parents worked very long hours when I was young, I spent a large part of my childhood there, much of it in the company of my aunt. Consequently she was a big influence on the way I grew up and on my sense of taste.

The bar and my aunt's house were filled with antiques and beautiful objects. When I look back, I see a world of grand pianos and huge gilt mirrors, of high ceilings and sumptuous velvet wall-hangings, a world where delicate Moroccan and Oriental influences mixed mysteriously with the darker, heavier textures of nineteenth-century Europe and of Weimar Germany. I particularly loved spending time in the changing room for the strippers and dancers, an exotic jungle of sequins and feathers, suffused with the rich fragrances of smoke and last night's perfume. Perhaps it was an unusual environment for a young girl, but to me it seemed perfectly normal, and I can now recognise that this atmosphere of everyday theatricality sowed the seeds for my later love-affair with Biba. When I first saw pictures of the interior of Biba, I could immediately identify with it – it was just like the Oasis on a grand scale.

At the time, of course, I knew nothing of Biba. And even when I moved from Berlin to London in the 1980s, my intention was to become a singer: the last thing on my mind was to become a collector of vintage clothing. I had little money in my pocket and – back then – all my belongings could fit comfortably in two suitcases with plenty of room to spare. It was September already, winter was coming on and, knowing there was no way I could afford the prices being charged in London boutiques, I needed to find a more affordable source for clothing. Which is when I first visited the market in Portobello Road in West London.

Portobello Road is best known as the largest antiques market in the world, so famous that thousands of tourists from dozens of countries descend upon it every Saturday in search of a bargain that they're extremely unlikely to find. Much more interesting to me, however, was the northern end of the market on a Friday morning, which attracted less attention and therefore settled for lower prices. This end of the market, where the cognoscenti outnumbered the tourists, still retained some of the rough-and-ready style of Portobello that had existed before gentility set in, a place where rag-and-bone men were more prevalent than antiques dealers, where amateurs and professionals worked side-by-side.

RIGHT: *Pari in Biba striped wool jersey trouser suit.*

history and style of an item. Initially I began to pick up pieces that attracted me by virtue of being both unusual and affordable. I was not then concerned with a particular label or even an era, though – perhaps unconsciously recalling the décor of Oasis – I found myself gravitating toward Art Deco: I remember, for example, a champagne-coloured cocktail dress from the twenties, with distinctive Deco wings to the shoulders and a diamanté-clasp belt, a stunning dress that I later sold to a museum.

And then one day my eye was caught by a jacket on a short tailor's dummy between the clothes rails on one particular stall. It was a very beautiful, brown, double-breasted jacket, fitted and with raised shoulders. It was most unusual, and I was drawn irresistibly to it. I walked all the way around the dummy, stopped and then walked back around the other way, almost spellbound. 'Of course, you know what this is?' said the stall-holder. I shook my head. 'This is a Biba jacket,' he explained, and he proceeded to give me a three-minute introduction to a label and a store and a dream that I had never previously encountered. Those three minutes changed my life. Because, having captured my imagination with a little of the background, he encouraged me to try the jacket on. And for the first time in my life I was wearing a garment that I truly felt was made for me, being a size 8. It hugged me so perfectly that I had no doubt that I was going to buy it, even though it was way beyond my price range. Without hesitation, I put down a deposit on that jacket, promising both the stall-holder and myself that every week I would go back to pay off

It opened up a whole new world to me, one that I entered enthusiastically. I had never studied fashion, but for anyone who cared to take an interest, Portobello Market was an education in itself. The huge range of periods and styles, from Victorian capes to outlandish contemporary club culture, could not fail to impress, and the knowledgeable stall-holders were always happy to talk about the

a bit more. It took me several weeks but eventually I was able to walk away with my first piece of Biba.

I began to look out for Biba, whilst still buying other items as well, and it wasn't long before I realised I had twelve pieces. A collection, I thought. Or at least, the start of a collection. I remember standing at my wardrobe and going through them one by one, fascinated by them, almost hypnotised by them. And it wasn't just the clothes, but the physical labels themselves that appealed to my love of Nouveau and Deco and that seemed to encapsulate so much of the atmosphere of the enterprise. I have since discovered that many others also fell in love with the label, and find even now that a single glimpse of those distinctive Biba logos can instantly trigger memories and associations.

I was now hooked and hungry for more garments, and other items would turn up. I would find a pair of shoes, for example, discovering to my surprise that Biba also made shoes and boots. Biba cosmetics turned up, then a Biba tea-caddy, leopard-skin print cushions, and more. And gradually the full enormity of this extraordinary endeavour began to dawn upon me.

I scoured Portobello Market every Friday, setting my alarm for five in the morning so I could get there while the stalls were still being set up. On winter mornings, I would turn up with a torch in my hand to help me see what was available. The rest of the week I spent searching other markets and vintage shops all over London to feed my new obsession. It was a time when Biba – indeed that whole era – was very unhip: demand was low and I stood out as someone with a peculiar but very persistent interest. I acquired the nickname 'the Biba Girl'. Most days were long and fruitless, but they were more than compensated for by the sporadic successes: if I found one piece of Biba, my buzz would last for days. It was becoming a passion, an addiction.

I began to advertise. I would ask for 'Biba clothes, boots, shoes, objects …' And I was amazed to find that people were phoning me up not because they had something to sell, but just because they wanted to talk about Biba, they wanted to reminisce. And those who did sell invariably had a story they wanted to tell, so that the simple act of buying a second-hand garment became a major social event. Many times I would arrange to meet someone to look at a piece, only for them to phone up at the last moment, full of apologies and explaining that they simply couldn't do it, they were unable to part with such a cherished possession. Even they, however, still wanted to talk about Biba and the importance it had in their lives.

Although I eventually studied the subject in a more academic manner, it was largely through these lovely women that I really learnt about Biba, that I came to understand its significance and recognise its unique place in British fashion. And it was through them too that I received a welcome reassurance: my obsession was not mine alone.

I would like to thank them, and I would like to dedicate this book – which illustrates much of my collection – to all the women I met who shared their Biba dream with me and who taught me about the Biba experience.

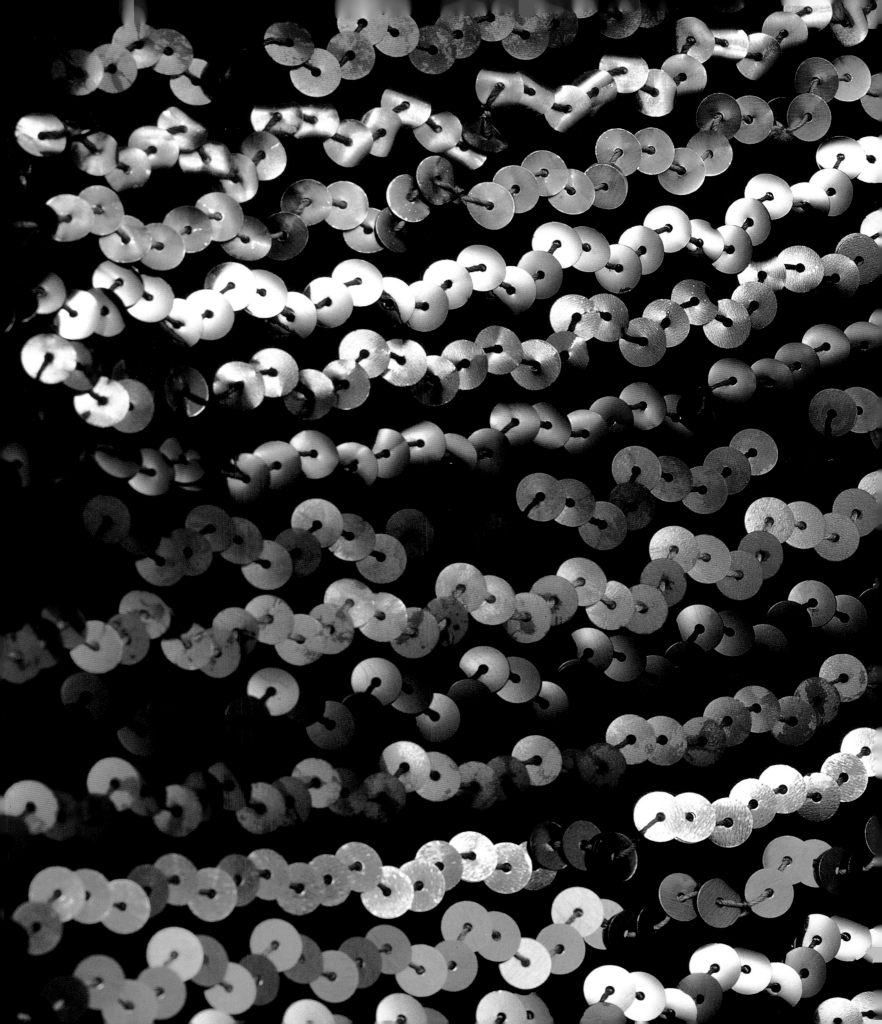

SHE'S A RAINBOW

HAVE YOU SEEN HER
ALL IN GOLD
JUST LIKE A QUEEN
IN DAYS OF OLD?

THE ROLLING STONES: 'SHE'S A RAINBOW

JAGGER/RICHARDS

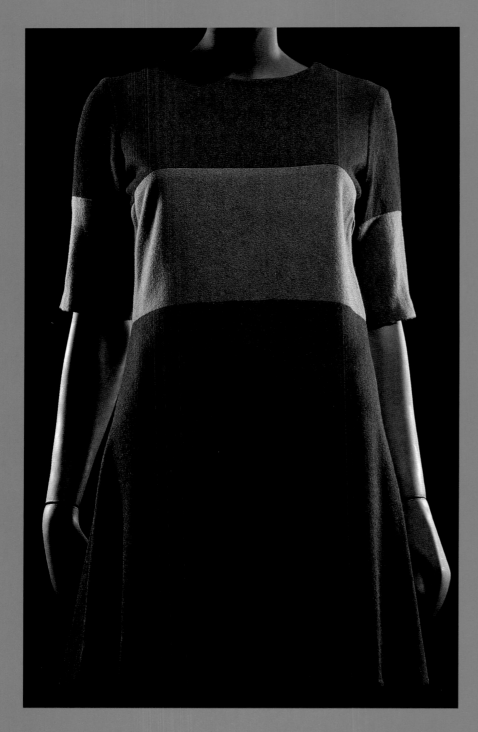

LEFT: *Wool A-line dress in black and brown, mid-1960s.*

OPPOSITE: *Outfit from mail-order catalogue: 'All wool pinafore dress with a low V-neck and cutaway back. A narrow bodice with a kick pleat at the front. Huntsman's blouse in satin. Softly billowing sleeves gathered high on the shoulder and into buttoned cuffs.' Prices: dress – £2 19s 6d; blouse – £3 3s 0d.*

LEFT: Four-colour wet-dye printed cotton mini-dress, mid-1960s. Fabric from Burgess & Ledward.

RIGHT: Empire-line, brushed cotton mini-dress with funnel neck, mid-1960s.

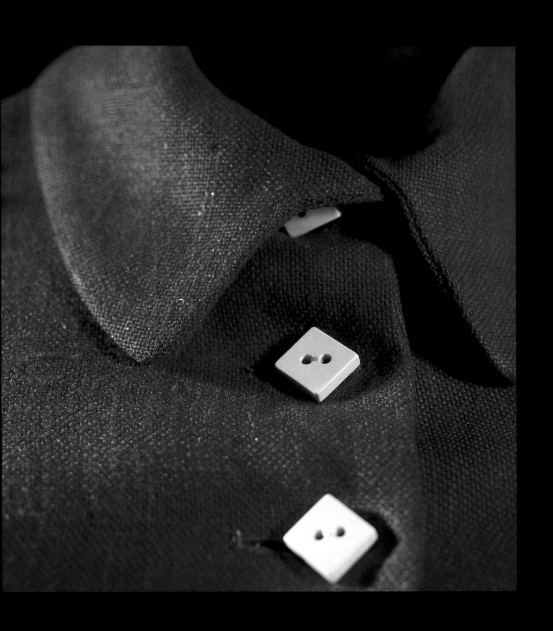

LEFT: *Vermillion, heavy, slubbed linen mix mini-dress with (below) diamond-shaped buttons. Mid-1960s.*

LEFT: *Orange, brushed cotton tunic dress with (right) gathered bell sleeve, mid-1960s.*

LEFT: *Cotton lawn mini-dress from mail-order catalogue (below). 'The dress has gathered sleeves gently billowing out to the elasticated cuffs, and a slashed neckline with a rounded edged open collar.'*

Model: Elizabeth Bjorn Neilson; photos: Harri Peccinotti.

Fine printed cotton set of 3 pieces. A bikini top with brief shorts that zip up the back. The dress has gathered sleeves gently billowing out to the elasticised cuffs, and a slashed neckline with a round edged open collar.

Colours White with pink flowers only.

Design number Price Dress 1A £3·3·0

Bikini 1B £2·10·0

Wool jersey mini-dress
with (right) juggler's sleeves
and side button-fastening
neck, mid-1960s.

RIGHT: *Midi-skirt with long-sleeved top, and mini-skirt suit, all in cotton jersey. Orange patent leather platform shoes and suede Biba boots.*

LEFT: *Detail of printed jersey fabric used in the midi-skirt.*

BELOW: *Cotton shirt dress, with panelled skirt, shoulder-pads and (right) signature heart-shaped buttons, late-1960s.*

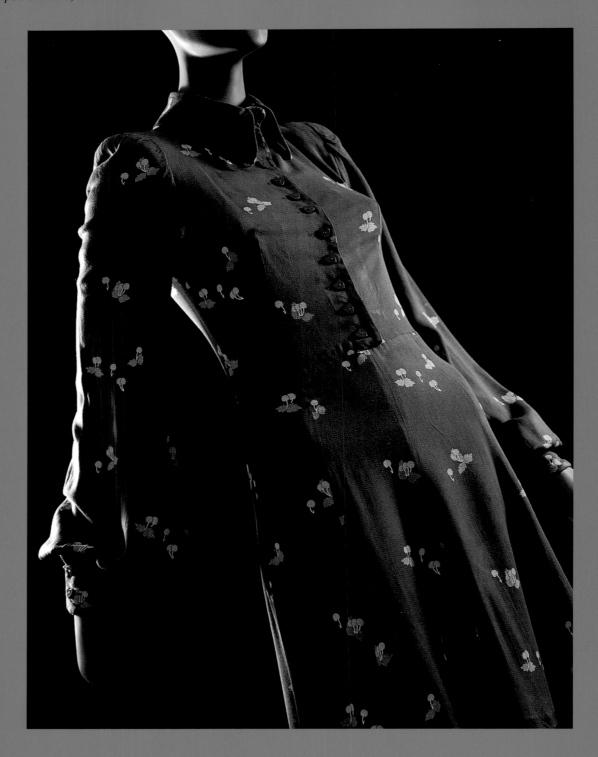

THIS PAGE: *Brushed cotton,
1930s-inspired print dress
with peplum, late-1960s.*

RIGHT: *Mycella maxi-dress
with wrap-over top and
flared skirt, early-1970s.
Fabric from Tootal's.*

FAR RIGHT: *Black-and-gold
lurex skirt suit with wrap
top, early-1970s.*

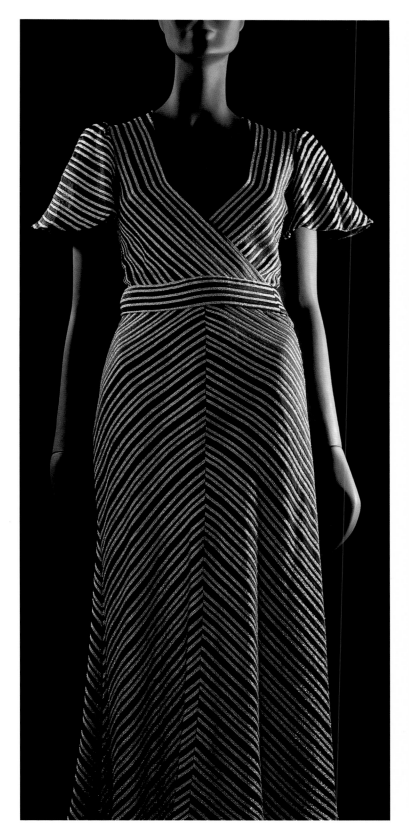

1940s-inspired brushed cotton dress with pieced skirt falling to full circle at the hem, and (right) shield breast-pocket and star-shaped buttons. Late-1960s.

LEFT: *Outfit from mail-order catalogue (below): 'Sleeveless jerkin and matching skirt in pure woven wool, the jerkin falling straight at the front with a cutaway back bodice. Unlined, faced with matching wool braiding. The skirt is high waisted with a kick pleat and fastens by the seven buttons. Colours: Mixed umber or dusty blue/grey.' Prices: jerkin – £2 10s 0d; skirt – £2 7s 6d. Model: Vicki Wise; photo: Hans Feurer; dog: Hannibal.*

D
Sleeveless jerkin
and matching skirt
in pure woven wool.
(Can be bought
separately).
The jerkin
falling straight at
the front with
a cutaway back bodice.
Unlined,
faced with matching
wool braiding.
Price:
£2·10·0

E
The skirt is
high waisted with a
kick pleat
and fastens by the
seven buttons.
Colours:
Mixed amber or
dusty blue/grey.
Price:
£2·7·6

F
Washable Flanesta
shirt in colours dyed
specially to
tone with the jerkin
and skirt.
It has a standaway
collar,
fly front with narrow
gathered sleeves.
Colours:
Cream, bay leaf brown
or dusty blue.
Price:
£2·17·6

G
Edwardian nightshirt
in washable Flanesta,
has a
high buttoned neck
and deep yoke.
The full sleeves
start on a
gathered shoulder
and end in long cuffs
fastened,
like the bodice,
with white
Mother of Pearl
buttons.
Colours:
Poppy red and
shell pink.
Price:
£4·19·6

BELOW LEFT: *Print dress with gathered batwing sleeves and leg-of-mutton cuffs, mid-1960s.*

BELOW RIGHT: *Cotton muslin dress with funnel collar, square yoke, batwing sleeves and leg-of-mutton cuffs, mid-1960s.*

RIGHT: *Cotton mix, sleeveless sundress with collar and patch pockets, alongside 1940s-inspired, cotton mix tea-dress with puffed sleeves. Both mid-1960s.*

Brushed cotton, poppy-print dress with stand collar, covered buttons and leg-of-mutton sleeves (left), mid-1960s.

LEFT: Cotton muslin summer dress with double-layer handkerchief sleeve and bound edges, mid-1970s.

RIGHT: Two clover-leaf printed maxi-dresses with back-ties. Left-hand dress in midnight blue with gathered cuffs, right-hand in raspberry with flared sleeves. Late-1960s.

BELOW: *Wrap around knitted sleeveless top with ties at the side. In the background is a three-quarter sleeved pull-on version with oval neck and deep cuffs.*

RIGHT: *Batwing crossover knit top with lurex stripe; extended ribbed cuffs and waistband, mid-1970s.*

BELOW: *Wool mix sweater with square neck and appliquéd strawberry motif, mid-1970s.*

RIGHT: *Wool mix sweater with cherry motif in Swiss embroidery, Raglan sleeves and accentuated 1940s cuffs and waist, mid-1970s.*

LEFT: *Wool jersey dress with spearpoint collar and featuring button panel with reversed grain, mid-1970s.*

RIGHT: *Nylon smock with silhouette floral pattern and gathered cuffs, early-1970s.*

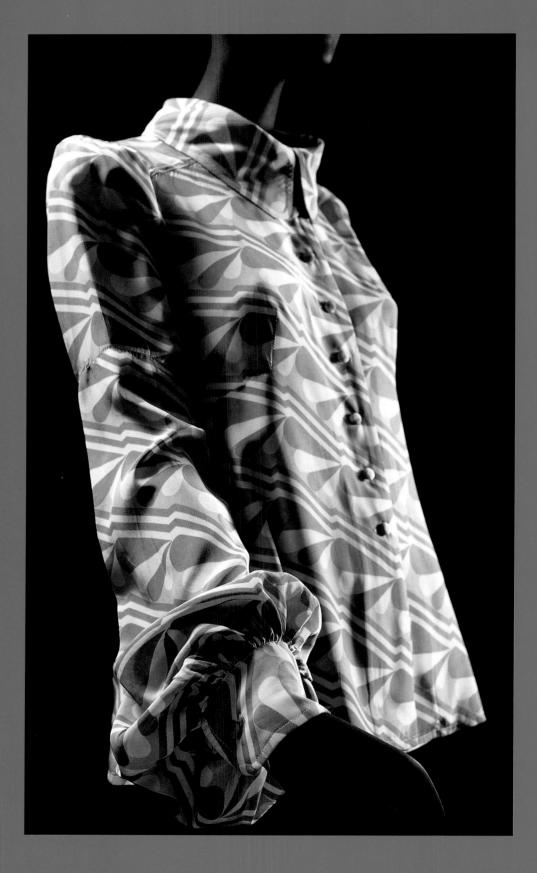

LEFT: *Rayon mini-dress with yoke and rounded collar; juggler's sleeves constructed in two pieces for extra fullness. Late-1960s.*

RIGHT: *Peacock green crushed panné velvet dress with side-zip fastening and covered buttons, late-1960s.*

*Tapestry maxi-waistcoat,
as worn by Barbara (p.50).
Late-1960s.*

LEFT: *Worsted wool skirt suit in deep mauve and cream with matching shaped choker. Flared midi skirt, jacket with peplum, covered buttons, tulip cuffs and separate belt, late-1960s.*

RIGHT: *Mixed fabric skirt suit, comprising flared skirt and jacket with peplum, satin-covered buttons and tulip cuffs, late-1960s.*

LEFT: *Detail from jersey-knitted knee-length coat.*

RIGHT: *Black linen suit: sleeveless dress and coat with bell sleeves. Early-1970s.*

Catalogue designed by John McColl
Models Donna Mitchell and Rosemari Johansson
Photographed by Sarah Moon
Hair by Leonard
Printed by Petro Press

THIS PAGE: *1940s-inspired lounge suit in satin; flared trousers with panty-line seam. Mid-1970s.*

RIGHT: *Two trouser suits from the late-1960s. Six-colour print with Eastern carpet motif and 32" flared trousers, and (far right) heavy, satin tonal damask-like print. Printed by IVO Prints.*

LEFT: *Cuffed trousers in jacquard jersey, early-1970s.*

RIGHT: *Straight, cropped trousers in linen with panty-line seam, and printed cotton flared trousers, early-1970s.*

LEFT: *Three-colour plated jersey knit trouser suit – ecru cat motif with apricot eyes on bitter chocolate. Jacket with patch pockets and pleated back, bag trousers falling to 34" bottoms.*

FAR RIGHT: *Synthetic, plated jersey mix suit in chequerboard pattern. Three-button jacket and 30" flares with 3" turn-ups. Mid-1970s.*

LEFT: *Suit from mail-order catalogue (below): 'Droopy coat in granny printed silky rayon with gored skirt, thirties trousers' (prices: coat – £3 10s 0d; trousers – £3 10s 0d), late-1960s. Brushed cotton mix flared trouser suit; jacket with pointed reveres and padded Raglan shoulders, mid-1970s. Catalogue models: Donna Mitchell and Ingemari Johanson; photo Helmut Newton.*

Droopy coat
in granny printed silky rayon
with gored skirt,
thirties trousers and
a 5½ foot long scarf.
The plain moss crepe blouse
has covered buttons
and matches the lighter
colour of the print.
For details of seaming on
the coat, see back page.

Colours
Prints
Black/Cream Navy/Red
Blouse
Cream or Red

Design Number
Price
Coat
F1
£3·10·0

Skirt
F2
£2· 2·0

Trousers
F3
£3·10·0

Blouse
F4
£3· 3·0

Scarf
F5
£1·12·6

Slinky hooded dress
in silky jersey,
can be worn
with floppy trousers.
The chain belt is oxidised
to look antique.

Colours
Burnt Orange
Hyacinth Blue
Black

Design Number
Price
Dress
G1
£3·15·6

Trousers
G2
£2·19·6

Belt
G3
£1· 9·6

See back page for
hood worn off the head

STREET LIFE

THIS BRAVE NEW WORLD'S
NOT LIKE YESTERDAY;
IT CAN TAKE YOU HIGHER
THAN THE MILKY WAY.

ROXY MUSIC: 'STREET LIFE'

BRYAN FERRY

LEFT: *Corduroy trench coat from mail-order catalogue (below) with 'many details including flap pockets, elbow patches, shirt collar and cuffs'. Fitted jacket with flounce at rear in tie-dyed cotton.*

Catalogue model: Stephanie Farrow; photos: Hans Feurer.

**Corduroy
Trench Coat and Skirt**

The coat is unlined
and has many details
including flap pockets,
elbow patches,
shirt collar and cuffs
and is belted and
buttoned down the front.
The elephant cord
is cut horizontally
and the flared skirt
is chevroned.
For exact details
of all garments
turn to the back page.

Colours
Pale Beige
Orchid Pink
Dusty Blue

Design number
Price
Coat
1A
£6·6·0

Skirt
1B
£2·10·0

LEFT: *1940s-inspired, bouclé wool fitted jacket with belt and square shoulders, early-1970s.*

RIGHT: *1940s-influenced wool jacket with faux-fur collar and cuffs featuring signature sleeve-head, mid-1970s.*

colours with matching hat,
mid-1960s; detail of fabric
shown opposite.

LEFT: *Deco-patterned wool jacquard jersey coat with faux-fur collar and cuffs, mid-1970s.*

RIGHT: *Burnt orange, cotton faux-fur coat with funnel neck, early-1970s.*

BELOW: *Zip-fastened faux-fur leopard-print jacket with peplum and faux-fur collar and cuffs, mid-1970s.*

RIGHT: *Open plaid winter maxi-coat with side-buttons and patch pockets, late-1960s.*

Deco-design skirt suit in three-colour jersey weave with faux-fur collar and cuffs. A-line maxi-skirt and (right) integral tie-waist to jacket, mid-1970s.

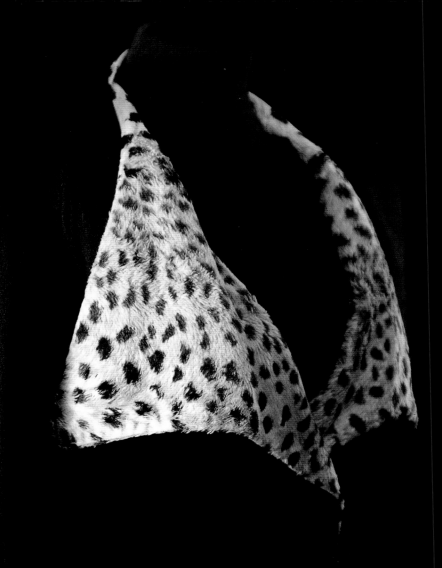

LEFT: *Full-length fitted coat in gabardine wool with patch pockets and detailed pocket flaps, early-1970s.*

RIGHT: *Wool jersey belted jacket with Raglan sleeve. The shark's fin collar and the cuffs are leopard-print faux-fur, early-1970s.*

LEFT: *Chalk-stripe coat with patch pockets and reveres, mid-1970s.*

BELOW: *A silver pen brooch with feather decoration. As with most of the jewellery sold at Biba, this was not designed by Barbara Hulanicki, but sourced from an outside supplier.*

LEFT: *1940s-inspired faux-fur swing-back coat in midnight blue, early-1970s.*

BELOW: *Knee-length A-line coat with flared sleeves, shawl collar, loop buttons and concealed pockets, late-1960s.*

LEFT: *Floor-length, crushed velvet coat with rounded collar, fitted waist and five-button fastening.*

RIGHT: *Faux-fur swing-back coat, with raised shoulders and pleated back (left), and full-length black faux-fur coat with roll collar and button detail on cuffs.*

BELOW: *Pair of faux-fur swing-back coats, with raised shoulders and pleated backs.*

RIGHT: *Tailored faux-fur double-breasted coat in leopard-skin print.*

FOLLOWING PAGES: *Cheetah-print faux-fur floor-length coat, mid-1970's.*

THE BIBA COLLECTION

LEFT: *Cheetah-print faux-fur floor-length coat, mid-1970s and double-breasted cotton velvet maxi-coat with covered buttons, late-1960s.*

BELOW: *Fitted jacket in wool jersey and lurex with pocket detail and single vent, mid-1970s.*

PUSS 'N' BOOTS

NOW YOU'RE WALKING LIKE
YOU'RE TEN FEET TALL.

NEW YORK DOLLS: 'PUSS 'N' BOOTS'

JOHANSEN/SYLVIAN

LEFT: *Thigh-high suede boots.*

BELOW: *1940s-inspired black suede ankle boots with faux-fur trim.*

LEFT: *Yellow patent l[...]*
platform shoes.

RIGHT: *Brown leather[...]*
platform shoes with
panel-heels.

BELOW: *Crepe 1920s-inspired shoes.*

RIGHT: *Canvas wedge-heeled boots.*

LEFT: *Two-toned leather shoes in cream and black.*

BELOW: *Grey suede shoes with ankle-straps.*

LEFT: *Knee-high suede boots.*

BELOW: *Blue suede high-heeled shoes.*

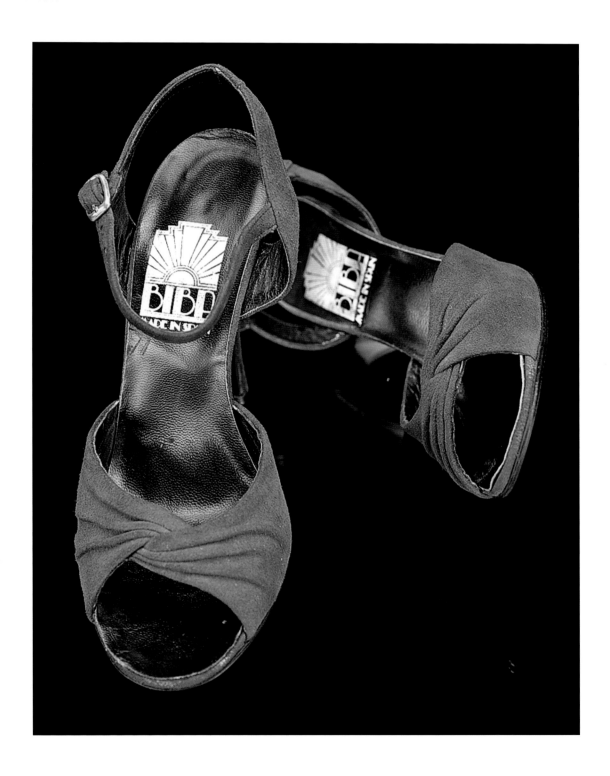

Two pairs of suede platform shoes with diamanté trim from the Lolita department at Big Biba in (below) red and (left) midnight blue.

CELLULOID HEROES

I WISH MY LIFE WAS A NON-STOP
HOLLYWOOD MOVIE SHOW.

THE KINKS: 'CELLULOID HEROES'

RAY DAVIES

BELOW: *Sequinned, stretched halter-neck top, mid-1970s.*

RIGHT: *Sequinned fitted jacket, mid-1970s.*

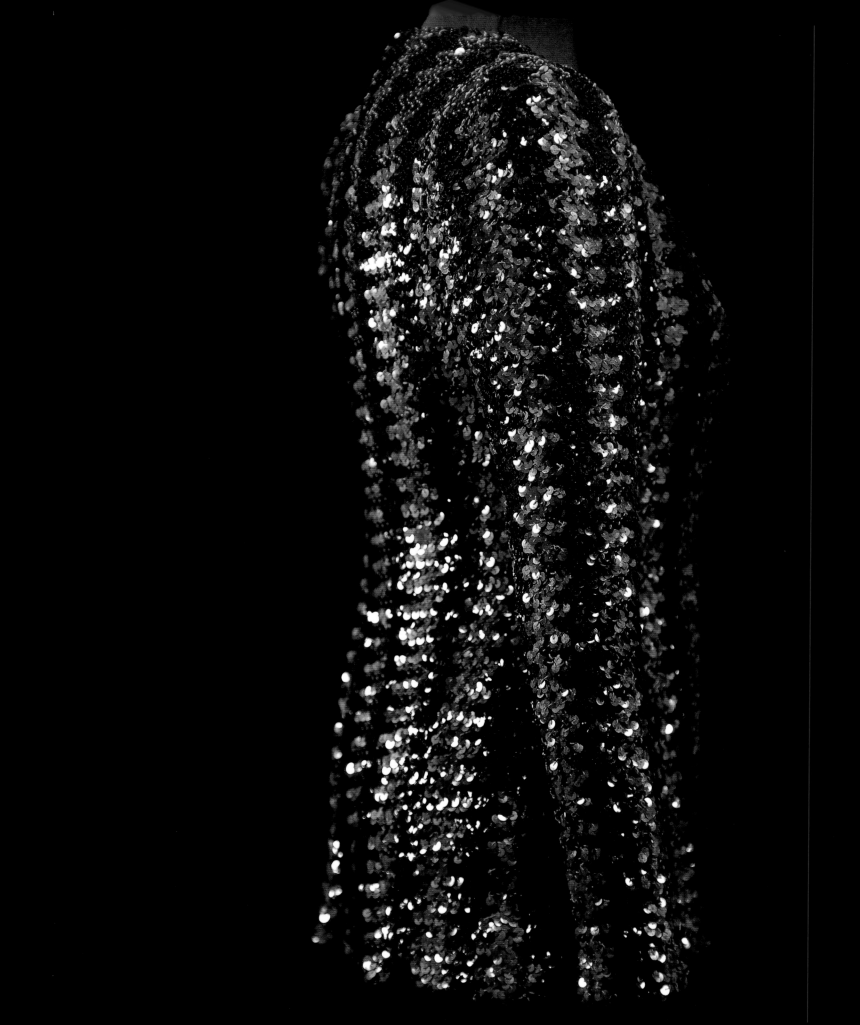

*Weave jacket gathered from
yoke with a pattern of birds
in flight (detail left) .*

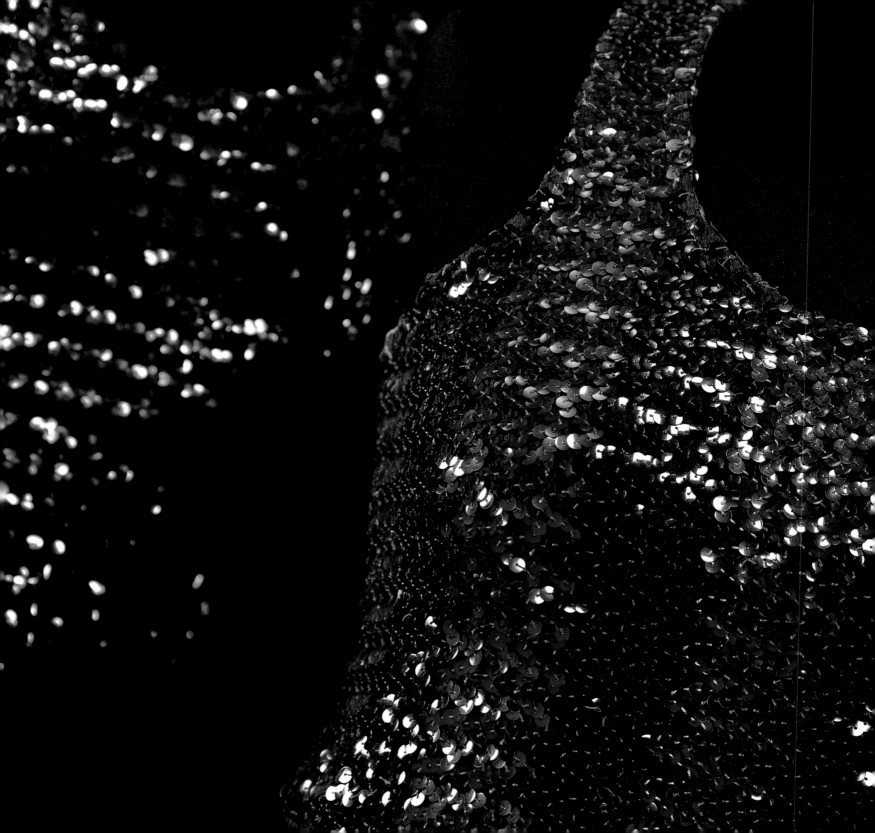

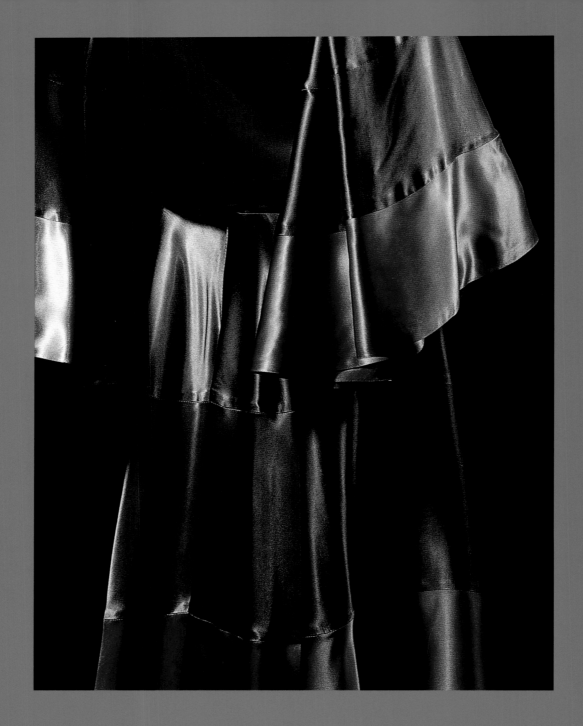

THE BIBA COLLECTION

LEFT: *1940s-style diamond-front, satin dress with gathered, raised cap sleeves, tie belt and concealed zip at back. Straight shape falling to below the knee, mid-1970s.*

RIGHT: *Black crepe dress with ruched cuffs, billowing sleeves gathered at the shoulder, half-back-tying belt and crepe-covered buttons. Falling to below knee-length in an open front, late-1960s.*

LEFT: *Loganberry crepe dress with cut-out front and covered seven-button cuffs, early-1970s.*

BELOW: *Wool mix jersey knit maxi-dress with ziggurat sequins and zipped back, mid-1970s.*

LEFT: *Detail of a long-sleeved dress in lurex thread, early-1970s.*

BELOW: *Lamé back-seamed trousers, early-1970s.*

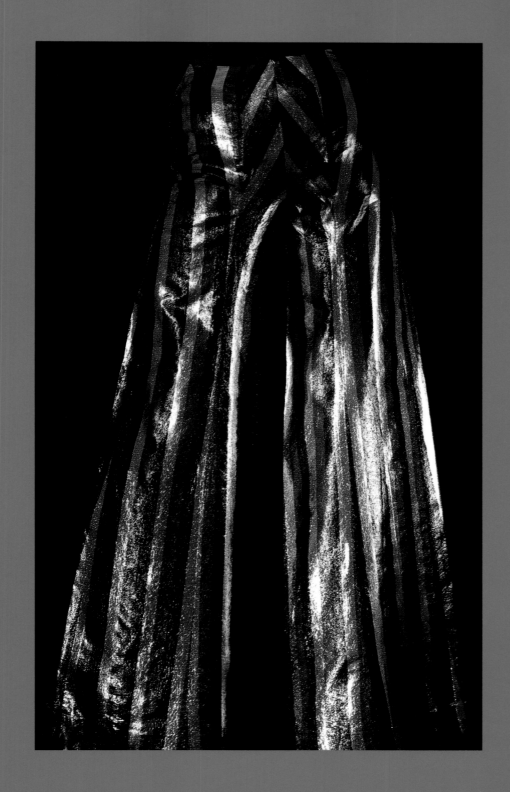

*Silk georgette dress with
plunging neckline and sheer
billowing sleeves, late-1960s,
with detail of embroidered
label (opposite).*

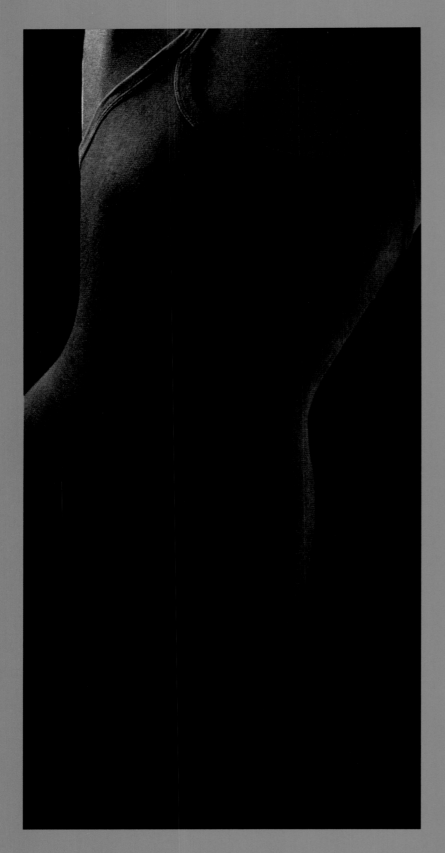

Pair of cotton jersey maxi-dresses with halter-neck.

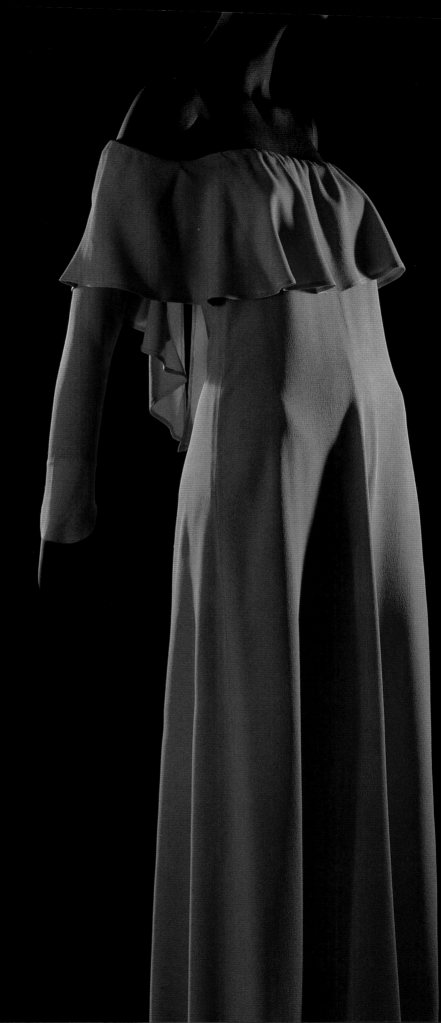

LEFT: *Empire-line crepe full-length evening dress with gathered raised shoulders, tapered sleeves, flared skirt, back-tie belt and zip to back, early-1970s.*

RIGHT: *Crepe full-length evening-dress with zipped three-quarter length sleeves, elasticated neckline and ruffle collar with points at the back, mid-1970s.*

LEFT: *Black crepe sleeveless dress, mid-1970s.*

BELOW: *Faux-fur tippet and teal-coloured maribou tippet, early-1970s.*

LEFT: *Pattern based on the Biba logo, early-1970s.*

RIGHT: *White lace, full-length wedding dress with handkerchief sleeves and Edwardian-style stand collar, early-1970s.*

LEFT: *Purple wool jersey flared evening dress with spaghetti straps and sequin neckline. Matching bolero jacket has fold-back collar with sequin trim and straight sleeves into elasticated sequinned cuffs, mid-1970s.*

RIGHT: *1940s-style black wool jersey skirt suit. Midi skirt, princess-line jacket with fold-back collar, sequin trim to lapels, buttons, angled pockets and slit skirt, mid-1970s.*

Black floor-length faux-fur cape, late-1960s, worn over a black sleeveless evening dress.

LEFT: *1940s-inspired satin
print house-coat.*

RIGHT: *Crepe kimono-style
dress with Deco print,
early-1970s.*

*Mail-order catalogue item:
'Edwardian nightshirt in
washable Flanesta, has a
high-buttoned neck and deep
yoke. The full sleeves start on
a gathered shoulder and end
in long cuffs, fastened like the
bodice with white
Mother of Pearl buttons.'
Price: £4 19s 6d.
Catalogue model Vicki Wise;
photos: Hans Feurer.*

D
Sleeveless jerkin
and matching skirt
in pure woven wool.
(Can be bought
separately).
The jerkin
falling straight at
the front with
a cutaway back bodice.
Unlined,
faced with matching
wool braiding.
Price :
£2·10·0

E
The skirt is
high waisted with a
kick pleat
and fastens by the
seven buttons.
Colours :
Mixed amber or
dusty blue/grey.
Price :
£2·7·6

F
Washable Flanesta
shirt in colours dyed
specially to
tone with the jerkin
and skirt.
It has a standaway
collar,
fly front with narrow
gathered sleeves.
Colours :
Cream, bay leaf brown
or dusty blue.
Price :
£2·17·6

G
Edwardian nightshirt
in washable Flanesta,
has a
high buttoned neck
and deep yoke.
The full sleeves
start on a
gathered shoulder
and end in long cuffs
fastened,
like the bodice,
with white
Mother of Pearl
buttons.
Colours :
Poppy red and
shell pink.
Price :
£4·19·6

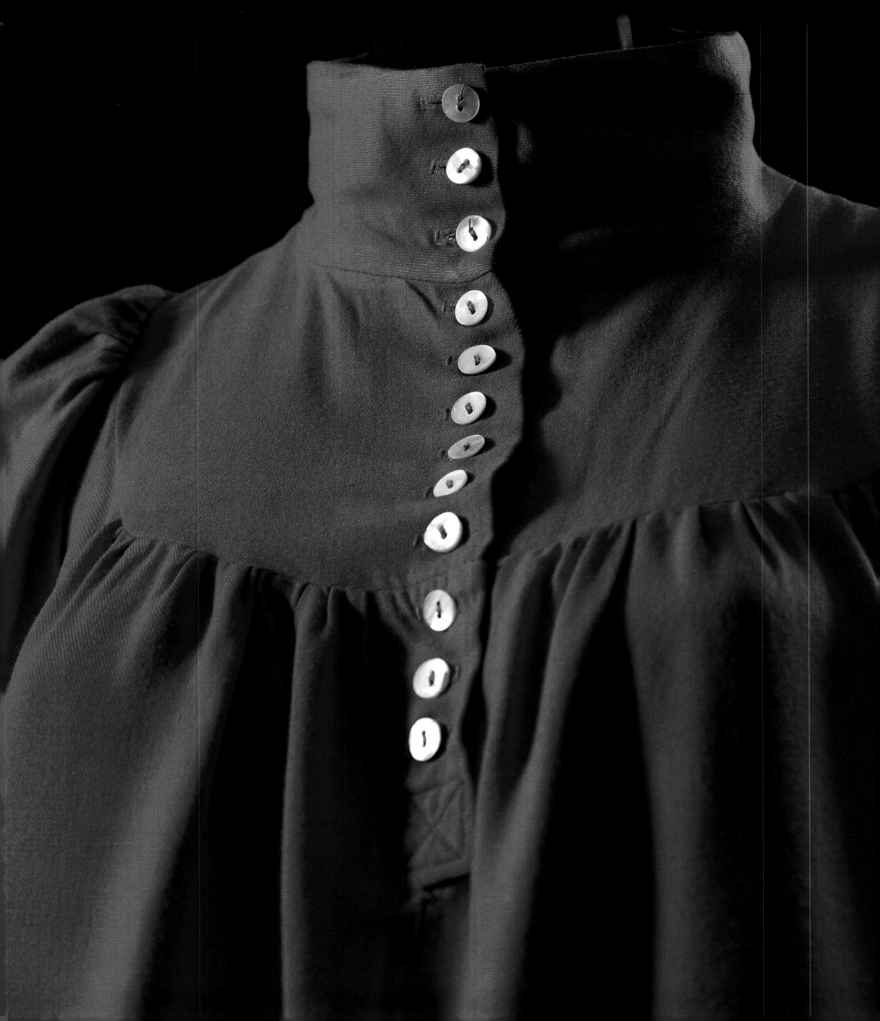

BELOW LEFT: *Satin coat with mermaid-tail sleeves, early-1970s.*

OPPOSITE: *Satin dressing gown with satin trim and signature puffed sleeves, mid-1970s.*

BELOW RIGHT: *Satin coffee-coloured pyjamas with shawl collar, mid-1970s.*

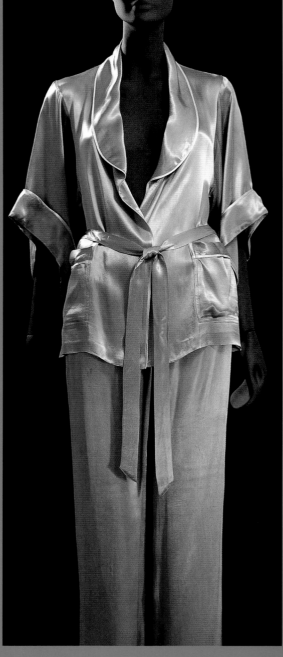

Two cheesecloth dresses with lace trim, layered sleeves, tied backs and tied cuffs. Buttermilk with sepia trim, and black with soft terracotta trim. Late-1960s.

BIBLIOGRAPHY

Apart from contemporary newspapers and magazines, as noted elsewhere, Biba has not been very well documented. The principal published account is, of course, Barbara Hulanicki's autobiography, *From A To Biba* (Hutchinson, London, 1983 – paperback edition: Comet, London, 1984). The only other figure from Biba to have published an autobiography is Tony Porter in *The Great White Palace* (Doubleday, London, 2002).

Two other vital works are *Biba: The Label, The Lifestyle, The Look* (Tyne & Wear Museum, Newcastle upon Tyne, 1993) and Kate McIntyre's 'Biba: Design, Identity and the Pleasure of Consumption' (unpublished MA thesis, Royal College of Art, London, 1994).

I am enormously indebted to Malcolm Bird, who provided me with the tape of an interview he and Brenda Lewis conducted with Barbara Hulanicki on 6 December 1966 for *Ark*, the magazine of the Royal College of Art.

Other books consulted include:

Nina Antonia, *Too Much, Too Soon: The Make-Up and Break-Up of the New York Dolls* (Omnibus, London, 1998)

Tony Benn, *Against the Tide: Diaries 1973–76* (pbk edn, Arrow, London, 1990)

Barbara Bernard, *Fashion in the 60s* (Academy Editions, London, 1978)

Cilla Black, *What's It All About?* (Ebury, London, 2003)

David Butler and Anne Sloman, *British Political Facts 1900–1979* (MacMillan, London, 1980)

Larry Eliott and Dan Atkinson, *The Age of Insecurity* (Verso, London, 1998)

Marnie Fogg, *Boutique: A '60s Cultural Phenomenon* (Mitchell Beazley, London, 2003)

Philippe Garner, *Sixties Design* (Taschen, Koln, 1996)

Boy George with Spencer Bright, *Take It Like A Man: The Autobiography of Boy George* (Sidgwick & Jackson, London, 1995)

Paul Gorman, *The Look: Adventures in Pop & Rock Fashion* (Sanctuary, London, 2001)

Jonathan Green, *All Dressed Up: The Sixties and the Counter-Culture* (Jonathan Cape, London, 1998)

Jonathon Green, *Days in the Life: Voices from the English Underground 1961–1971* (pbk edn, Pimlico, London, 1998)

Jennifer Harris, Sarah Hyde and Greg Smith, *1966 and All That: Design and the Consumer 1960–1969* (Trefoil, London, 1986)

Amy de la Haye (ed.), *Fashion Source Book* (Macdonald Orbis, London, 1988)

Hermione Hobhouse (gen. ed.), *Survey of London Vol XLII: Southern Kensington* (Athlone Press, London, 1986)

Barney Hoskyns, *Glam: Bowie, Bolan and the Glitter Rock Revolution* (Faber, London, 1998)

Georgina Howell (ed.), *In Vogue: Six Decades of Fashion* (Allen Lane, London, 1975)

Lesley Jackson, *The Sixties: Decade of Design Revolution* (Phaidon, London, 1998)

Edward Jones and Christopher Woodward, *A Guide to the Architecture of London* (Weidenfeld & Nicholson, London, 1983)

George Melly, *Revolt Into Style: The Pop Arts in Britain* (pbk edn, Penguin, Harmondsworth, 1972)

Molly Parkin, *Good Golly Ms Molly* (Star, London, 1978)

Mary Quant, *Quant by Quant* (Cassell, London, 1966)

Jon Savage, *England's Dreaming: Sex Pistols and Punk Rock* (pbk edn, Faber & Faber, London, 1992)

Twiggy, *Twiggy: An Autobiography* (Hart-Davies MacGibbon, London, 1975)

Twiggy, *In Black and White: An Autobiography* (Simon & Schuster, London, 1997)

Tom Vague, *Anarchy in the UK: The Angry Brigade* (AK Press, Edinburgh, 1997)

Linda Watson, *Vogue: Twentieth Century Fashion* (Carlton, London, 1999)

REFERENCES

Much of the material in the text derives from interviews conducted by telephone or in person, or from email correspondence, during 2003; these personal communications are indicated in the following notes by (pc). Publication details of books are given in the bibliography. All newspapers and magazines are London publications, unless otherwise stated.

CHAPTER 1: The In Crowd

P.6 **most beautiful store** – *Draper's Record*, quoted in *Sunday Times* magazine, 28 September 1975; **in the armchair booths** – *Kensington News & Post*, 26 September 1975; **grave robbery … old friend** – Debby Faulkner-Stevens (pc); **like someone dying** – *The Times*, 20 August 1975; **watching everything go** – *Evening News*, 12 September 1975

P.8 **Superstore Boutique** – *Sunday Telegraph*, 9 September 1973; **Harrods and Macey's** – *Sunday Times* 9 September 1973; **friend's bedroom** – Genevieve Williams (pc); **end of a dream** – Tony Benn, *Against the Tide* p.421

P.9 **huge part of us growing up** – Michelle Coomber (pc); **election in May 1979** – Clare Hoffman (pc); **lamb dressed as mutton** – *Punch*, 21 September 1983; **word had not then been used** – see Marnie Fogg, *Boutique* p. 7. The following two paragraphs also draw on the same book.

P.10 **things started to hot up** – *ibid*. p.35; **born on 8 December** – much of the following section is derived from Barbara Hulanicki, *From A To Biba*

P.11 **bright colours were vulgar** – Barbara Hulanicki, *From A To Biba* p.36; **a huge influence on the Biba look** – *Sunday Telegraph* magazine, 6 May 1990; **four years solid drawing … possibly do** – Brenda Lewis and Malcolm Bird interviewing Barbara Hulanicki for *Ark*, December 1966 (see Bibliography)

P.12 **high turnover** – Kate McIntyre, *Biba* p.19; **twenty-five bob** – *Daily Mirror*, 4 May 1964; **cocktail party** – Mary Quant, quoted in Harris, Hyde and Smith *1966 and All That* p.55; **upper class women in Chelsea** – George Melly (pc)

P.13 **clothes for kept women** – *The Late Show*, 22 February 1993, quoted in Kate McIntyre, *op. cit.* p.15; **just as a hobby** – Lewis and Bird *op. cit.*; **misgivings of Fitz** – Lewis and Bird *op. cit.*; **loan of £2,000** – *Sunday Times* magazine, 28 September 1975; **rent of £20** – Kate McIntyre, *op. cit.* p.23

P.14 **very crude, very basic** – John McConnell (pc); **French boutiques** – Kate McIntyre, *op. cit.* p.25; **Ali Baba** – Kate McIntyre, *op. cit.* p.29; **girl's place of secret passion** – John McConnell (pc); **someone's house … restaurant** – Olivia Temple (pc); **he doesn't want to know** – Lewis and Bird *op. cit.*

P.15 **I couldn't stand those old bags** – *Evening Standard*, 23 September 1975; **Can I help you, madam** – Barbara Hulanicki, *From A To Biba* p.81; **men turned up with their girlfriends** – Simon Jenkins (pc); **uber-dolly** –
Jonathon Green, *All Dressed Up* p.79

P.16 ***Ready Steady Go!* was the showcase** – John McConnell (pc); **Mary Quant's clothes … trendy** – Sarah Burnett (pc); **little-girly shapes** – Olivia Temple (pc); **youngsters loved our stuff** – *Time Out*, 28 March 1990; **If you didn't buy what you wanted** – Twiggy, *In Black and White* p.43; **How many times a year** – John McConnell (pc); **a place of pilgrimage** – *Evening News*, 16 September 1969; **There was this amazing delivery** – Sarah Burnett (pc)

P.18 **enormously aware of colour and design** – quoted in Lesley Jackson, *op. cit.* p.36; **It didn't intimidate** – George Melly (pc); **The mothers of the girls** – *Time Out*, 28 March 1990; **'London: the most exciting city in the world'** – feature by John Crosby, *Daily Telegraph*, 16 April 1965; **'Society: The Index'** – *Queen*, July 1965; **the most In shop for gear** – *Time* (New York, USA), 15 April 1966

P.19 **Cavern Club darkness** – *Evening News*, 16 September 1969; **feeling of boudoir** – Sheila Ruskin (pc); **she didn't want to sell** – Anthea Davies (pc); **one's relationship with a room** – *House & Garden*, February 1968; **most exotic shop in London** – *Vanity Fair*, October 1968

P.20 **saw some of her work** – *Evening Standard*, 18 August 1966; **I believe now that** – George Melly, *Revolt Into Style* p.134

P.22 **I admire Beardsley … vagueness in art** – *Women's Wear Daily* (New York, USA), 15 December 1966; **Aubrey Beardsley jungles** – *Evening Standard*, 18 August 1966; **Art Nouveau is never still** – quoted in Kate McIntyre *op. cit.* p.37; **Barbara bought some cologne** – John McConnell (pc); **the 1890s style of Liberty** – Catherine McDermott: The Biba Logo – The First Designer Lifestyle, in *Biba: The Label, The Lifestyle, The Look* pp.16–17; **If Biba had failed** – John McConnell (pc); **everyone under 30** – *Evening News* 16 September 1969

P.23 **Keith used to steal my clothes** – *Marie Claire*, June 2002; **Whoever came to England** – Rosie Young (pc); **One day I was in my little room** – Anthea Davies (pc)

P.24 **Four of us from Biba** – Sarah Burnett (pc); **I met Raquel Welch** – *Mail on Sunday*, 4 January 2004; **he asked me if I knew a shop** – Twiggy, *An Autobiography* pp.25-26; **a mixture of thirties** – Antony Little (pc)

P.25 **a name synonymous with … candlelight** – *Daily Mail*, 14 August 1967; **slithery gowns in glowing satins** – Jonathon Green, *All Dressed Up* p.79; **There had always been a twenties air** – Twiggy, *In Black and White* p.43; **Old, in our view** – Eleanor Powell (pc); **the wrong people** – Lewis and Bird *op. cit.*; **I love Barbara Hulanicki's clothes** – *Vanity Fair*, October 1968; **the pound sterling** – *Women's Wear Daily* (New York, USA), 15 December 1967

P.26 **People went up into their attics** – George Melly (pc); **shopping without cynicism** – Linda Watson, *Vogue: Twentieth Century Fashion* p.100; **I'm all for a child** developing – *House & Garden*, February 1968; **zinging tomato red** – *Women's Wear Daily* 15 December 1966; **we couldn't afford** – John McConnell (pc); **cylindrical capsule-shaped changing rooms** – Lesley Jackson, *op. cit.* p.36; **It's getting much better** – Lewis and Bird *op. cit.*

P.27 **I'd be hanging round the shop** – Anthea Davies (pc); **remembers confronting one customer** – Eleanor Powell (pc); **This girl came up to me** – Sheila Ruskin (pc)

P.28 **Fitz was to insist** – quoted in Kate McIntyre *op. cit.* p.29; **more turnover per square foot** – *Evening News* 16 September 1969; **I felt extremely nervous** – *You* magazine, 31 January 1993; **sowing the seeds of its own ruin** – *Times Literary Supplement* 21 October 1983; **there was a sense of urgency** – Sarah Burnett (pc); **Someone told us that Biba** – Lesley Garner (pc); **We were the epitome** – Lesley Garner, quoted in *Sunday Times* (Johannesburg, South Africa), 30 May 1999

P.29 **Brighton wasn't quite so much on the ball** – Rosie Young (pc); **It involves so much personal attention** – Lewis and Bird *op. cit.*; **We didn't do 16s** – Eleanor Powell (pc)

P.30 **Annie was wonderful** – Shirley Shurville (pc); **It was her cuts** – Eleanor Powell (pc); **everything was different** – Catherine Ross: 'Biba, Black Dwarf, Black Magic Women' in *Biba: The Label, The Lifestyle, The Look* p.13 **horrid drawings** – John McConnell (pc); **create the atmosphere** – quoted in Catherine McDermott: The Biba Logo – The First Designer Lifestyle, in *Biba: The Label, The Lifestyle, The Look* p.18; **When I meet my boyfriend** – John McConnell (pc); **we couldn't afford** – John McConnell (pc)

P.31 **Jinty ... Mary Quant** – prices from *Daily Mail*, 2 September 1969; **It was a very low salary** – Tony Porter, *The Great White Palace* p.48; **we were just swamped** – Tony Porter (pc)

P.33 **they got this thing** – John McConnell (pc); **didn't stand up to the post** – Tony Porter (pc); **I bought a beautiful tweed trouser suit** – Anna Ludlow (pc); **a halo of golden ringlets** – Barbara Hulanicki, *From A To Biba* p.98; **people who couldn't get to London** – John McConnell (pc); **things started to go badly wrong** – Tony Porter, *The Great White Palace* p.50; **about three thousand cheques** – Tony Porter (pc)

CHAPTER 2: Oh, You Pretty Things
P.34 **something of the glamour and glitter** – *Sunday Telegraph*, 9 September 1973; **a velvet trouser suit** – prices from *Evening Standard*, 17 September 1969; **April Ashley opened her restaurant** – April Ashley (pc)

P.37 **a curious area** – Antony Little (pc); **concept of the Biba car** – Steve Thomas (pc)

P.38 **Nearly every girl had a pair** – Trevor Sorbie (pc); **That excited us** – *Independent*, 12 February 1993; **There was an absolute fight** – Tony Porter (pc); **75,000 pairs of the boots** – Barbara Hulanicki, *From A To Biba* p.116; **30,000 of them** – Lesley Jackson, *op. cit.* p.44; **annual turnover of £200** – *Financial Times*, 11 September 1973

P.39 **a delivery of clothes** – Kate McIntyre, *op. cit.* p.73; **He was a good businessman ... marvellous** – Ellen Haas (pc); **One of the difficulties** – Antony Little (pc); **There were Edwardian jam-pots** – Anthea Davies (pc); **Every two hours or so** – Rosie Young (pc); **We were all very badly paid ... found things** – Daphne Bewes (pc)

P.40 **Oh yes, I'd like to do anything** – Lewis and Bird *op. cit.*; **Kensington is a darned awkward area** – Kate McIntyre, *op. cit.* p.40

P.41 **a voluptuous Mae West figure** – *Observer*, 20 July 1975; **She did have some strange ideas** – Daphne Bewes (pc); **the lads just thought** – Caroline Imlah: 'Designer Fashion, Street Style' in *Biba: The Label, The Lifestyle, The Look* p.7; **There had never been anything** – Karen Rymer (pc)

P.42 **I'm not sure we got it terribly right** – Daphne Bewes (pc); **She was the nearest thing** – Daphne Bewes (pc)

P.44 **the demand was so great** – Norma Kamali (pc); **There was no tradition of Biba windows** – Steve Thomas (pc); **70-year-old citadel of elegance ... modern retailing** – Bergdorf Goodman press release, 4 February 1971

P.46 **they were going to do the manufacturing** – Shirley Shurville (pc); **they absolutely backed us** – Shirley Shurville (pc)

P.47 **You have only five minutes ... a violent explosion** – *The Times*, 3 May 1971; **Half the basement** – Barbara Hulanicki, *From A To Biba* p.117; **The shop is closing** – Debby Faulkner-Stevens (pc); **Fascism and oppression will be smashed** – Tom Vague, *Anarchy in the UK* p.34. Much of the information here about the Angry Brigade draws on the same book; **Biba's concern with fashion** – Catherine Ross: 'Biba, Black Dwarf, Black Magic Women' in *Biba: The Label, The Lifestyle, The Look* p.13

P.48 **Communique #8** – Tom Vague *op. cit.* p.51; **way-out militant women** – *Evening Standard*, 3 May 1971; **women must be young** – 'No More Miss America', press release, 1968; **if you go on with this** – *Guardian*, 26 November 2001

P.49 **macabre tribute ... deco-decadence** – *Guardian*, 19 July 1975

P.50 **Angry Brigade Mk.II Hits Biba** – *Spare Rib*, November 1972; **USDAW** – Union of Shop, Distributive and Allied Workers; **For an eight hour day** – *Spare Rib*, October 1972; **You'd really feel proud** – Dizzy Thorne (pc); **to work there was special** – Yvette Barnett (pc)

P.51 **Biba was a close-knit community** – Bob White (pc) **livid** – *Guardian*, 23 February 1973; **an eleventh hour decision** – Bob White (pc); **the best branch I ever had** – Bob White (pc); **a deputation approached Fitz-Simon** – *Sunday Times* magazine, 28 September 1975; **Guerrillas of Great Britain** – Barbara Hulanicki, *From A To Biba* p.117; **I was inside a changing room** – Toni Franklin (pc)

CHAPTER 3: Cabaret
P.52 **It sounds a big jump** – *The Times*, 1 December 1971; **used to go past it** – *Financial Times*, 11 September 1973; **It was so beautiful ... splendour** – Barbara Hulanicki, *From A To Biba* p.125; **dating back to the Toms family grocery** – see Hermione Hobhouse, *Survey of London*, from where the information in this paragraph is derived.

P.54 **A large dull rectangle** – Jones and Woodward, *A Guide to the Architecture of London* p.151; **seems to be quite modern** – *Building*, May 1933; **one of the best examples of indirect lighting** – *The Architect & Building News*, 14 April 1933; **such masterpieces as the Chrysler Building** – *New Yorker* (New York, USA), 18 February 1974; **Do you realise ... that way** – *Daily Telegraph*, 7 February 1972

P.55 **By the time it closed** – *New Yorker* (New York, USA), 18 February 1974; **The only thing that was amazing** – Sheila Ruskin (pc); **the best high tea on Kensington High Street** – Angie Bowie (pc); **Derry & Toms is best known** – *Vogue*, June 1969

P.57 **the greatest gamble of her career** – *Sunday Times*, 9 September 1973; **Because the brand was so strong** – Steve Thomas (pc)

P.58 **She thought it was great** – Steve Thomas (pc); **a very** loose outline brief – *Building Design*, 25 July 1975; **I used to see Barbara Hulanicki** – Kasia Charko (pc); **they used to work like crazy** – Anthea Davies (pc); **seven days and seven nights** – Shirley Shurville (pc); **working seven days a week** – *Building Design*, 25 July 1975

P.59 **A lot of people would go in and help** – Malcolm Bird (pc); **almost Hollywood environment** – *Building Design*, 25 July 1975; **the core of the old Biba** – Steve Thomas (pc)

P.61 **a rich idiot buying up all the hat stands** – Barbara Hulanicki, *From A To Biba* p.113; **more than 200 such pieces** – 'Goodbye Ken High!' Bonham's auction catalogue, 4 October 1975; **Egyptian changing rooms** – *Building Design*, 25 July 1975; **intended to make expectant mothers** – *Sunday Telegraph*, 9 September 1973

P.62 **What age do you want … this wall** – *Building Design*, 25 July 1975; **to keep the youngsters amused** – *Sunday Telegraph*, 9 September 1973; **there are dressing gowns** – *Sunday Times*, 9 September 1973; **real fur in 1967** – Lewis and Bird *op. cit.*; **ivory-topped canes** – *Sunday Times*, 9 September 1973; **a lush, pink, Hollywood-style bedroom** – *Sunday Telegraph*, 9 September 1973; **frilled plastic boxes** – *Sunday Times*, 9 September 1973; **Thank Christ you've kept it** – *Building Design*, 25 July 1975; **preserved intact** – *Sunday Telegraph*, 9 September 1973; **they all 'remember' it** – *Building Design*, 25 July 1975

P.64 **a skinny black skyscraper** – *Sunday Times*, 9 September 1973; **They packaged everything with a Biba logo** – Mark Eastment (pc); **We were going to do a fish-and-chip shop** – Steve Thomas (pc)

P.66 **a 150-seater cinema** – *Daily Telegraph*, 7 February 1972; **a place where people can relax** – *Sunday Telegraph*, 9 September 1973; **on the ground floor alone** – *Sunday Times* magazine, 28 September 1975

P.68 **a more mature relationship** – *New Yorker* (New York, USA), 18 February 1974; **seven floors of retail** – Steve Thomas (pc); **the first time that anyone in this country** – *Daily Mail*, 11 September 1969; **you bought into the brand** – Steve Thomas (pc)

P.69 **the sheer scope of the enterprise** – *Evening Standard*, 10 September 1973; **a palace of apricot marble** – *Vogue*, 15 September 1973; **the most beautiful department store** – *Sunday Mirror*, 9 September 1973; **we wish her well** – *Sunday Times*, 9 September 1973

P.70 **It's a natural progression really** – *Sunday Telegraph*, 9 September 1973; **We will need to convert sightseers … age bracket** – *Evening Standard*, 10 September 1973; **one of the biggest gambles** – *Financial Times*, 11 September 1973; **I was told nine years ago** – *Sunday Telegraph*, 9 September 1973

P.71 **By eleven o'clock that morning** – Shirley Shurville (pc); **a black woman washing white clothes** – Steve Thomas (pc)

P.75 **a gang of murderous queens** – Nina Antonia, *Too Much Too Soon*, p.84; **All these people got dressed up** – Barney Hoskyns, *Glam!* p.86; **Why are you playing Biba's** – Nina Antonia, *op. cit.* p.105

P.76 **They ripped us off bow-legged** – Shirley Shurville (pc); **Arthur tried on a black jacket** – Nina Antonia, *op. cit.* p.104; **the attitude of pilfering** – Ian Dickson (pc); **They were all drunk** – Kasia Charko (pc); **They were perfect** – Mick Rock (pc); **They were amazing** – Adam Ant (pc); **It was a very hip statement** – Mick Rock (pc); **the glam party centre** – Mick Rock (pc); **the hallowed Mecca of the near-decadent** – *Melody Maker*, 11 October 1975; **Screaming Lord Sutch** – Graham Sharp

(pc); **the outrageously camp Rainbow Room** – *Record & Radio Mirror*, 9 February 1974; **It was very stilted** – Dave Pearce (pc); **It took away the untouchable aspect** – Dizzy Thorne (pc)

P.77 **He adored the store** – Barbara Hulanicki, *From A To Biba* p.146; **Angie and I had both seen the book** – *Mirabelle*, 6 October 1973, under Bowie's name but almost certainly written by Cherry Vanilla; **I loved the store … I was one** – Angie Bowie (pc)

P.78 **It's really a beautiful shop** – *Circus*, April 1975; **a drag queen undergoing hormone treatment** – Boy George, *Take It Like A Man*, p.92; **That was a wild affair** – Mick Rock (pc); **The Roof Garden was where you** – Debby Faulkner-Stevens (pc); **Walk into the new Biba** – *Evening News*, 10 September 1973; **like a strange Disneyland** – Sarah E Edgson (pc); **like walking into Narnia** – Michelle Coomber (pc); **the cold reality of the street** – Molly Parkin, *The Late Show*, 22 February 1993, quoted in Kate McIntyre, *op. cit.* p.43; **fantasy for the night** – Steve Thomas (pc); **The lifts, when they were working** – Anna Ludlow (pc)

P.79 **Roxy Music's new single** – Marco Perroni (pc); **invited to design the costumes** – *Evening News*, 1 September 1975; **like a Busby Berkeley film set** – *Observer*, 20 July 1975; **almost a fringe activity** – Alistair Best, *Design*, quoted in de la Haye, *Fashion Source Book*, p.147; **a suicidal gamble** – Alistair Best, *Design*, quoted in Anne Massey: 'Biba – Interior Lifestyles' in *Biba: The Label, The Lifestyle, The Look* p.24; **go to the Rainbow Room** – Michelle Coomber (pc); **just liked sitting in the window** – Kate George (pc) **the overwhelming theatricality** – *Sydney Morning Herald* (Sydney, Australia), 12 August 2003; **it was slightly dangerous** – Clare Hoffman (pc); **I'd never seen so many people** – Sarah E Edgson (pc)

P.80 **We'd get off the train** – Debby Faulkner-Stevens (pc); **spent the whole day at Biba** – Peter Westcott (pc); **Towards the end of the day** – Anna Ludlow (pc); **I was working in a bank in the City** – Dizzy Thorne (pc); **they thought I was some kind of criminal** – Yvette Barnett (pc); **I was totally mind-blown** – Wendy Faehse (pc); **It wasn't like working** – Yvette Barnett (pc); **quite difficult to buy stuff** – Debby Faulkner-Stevens (pc); **it took you half an hour** – Anna Ludlow

P.81 **cheap but original dolly bird fashion** – *Guardian*, 11 September 1973; **a pair of snakeskin shoes** – prices from *Cosmopolitan*, October 1974; **The size and the space just didn't suit it** – Sheila Ruskin (pc); **Although it wasn't a secret** – George Melly (pc); **very much the early ones** – Olivia Temple (pc); **Everything looks like an imitation** – *The Times*, 11 September 1973; **It was our introduction to the surreal** – Clare Hoffman (pc)

CHAPTER 4: Tumbling Down

P.82 **£3.9m** – *The Times*, 9 June 1973; **That's the end of us** – *Sunday Times* magazine, 28 September 1975; **We were just very unlucky** – *Time Out*, 28 March 1990; **so helpful** – Shirley Shurville (pc); **We were interested in real estate** – John Ritblat (pc); **a million visitors a week** – *Observer*, 20 July 1975; **This week has been simply tremendous** – *Newsweek* (New York, USA), 24 September 1973

P.84 **We used to sit there** – Shirley Shurville (pc)

P.85 **one of Britain's fastest growing … £1.75m** – *The Times*, 26 April 1973; **a millionaire by the age of 33** – *Sunday Telegraph*, 18 June 1995; **eschews neither risk nor controversy** – *The Times*, 26 April 1973; **if market values fall** – *The Times*, 26 April 1973; **heavily supported by its bankers** – *Observer*, 20 July 1975;

122p – *Financial Times*, 22 August 1974; **just 12p** – *Daily Mail*, 18 September 1974; **rumours that British Land** – *Guardian*, 20 September 1974; **further rumours** – *Western Mail*, 20 September 1974; **a fundamental disagreement** – unissued Biba press release dated 18 July 1974; **The present situation … implementation and action** – letter dated 29 October 1974 from David Roxburgh to Mr and Mrs SC Fitz-Simon; **With great regret for the past** – unsent letter dated November 1974 from BS and SC Fitz-Simon to David Roxburgh

P.87 **This is a temporary closure** – *Guardian*, 8 March 1975; **months of demoralising gossip** – *The Times*, 5 August 1975; **It was a nightmare** – Daphne Bewes (pc); **Dorothy Perkins launched themselves** – Shirley Shurville (pc)

P.88 **The whole atmosphere changed** – Wendy Faehse (pc); **Everywhere in the store … tins had done** – *Sunday Times* magazine, 28 September 1975; **all the bums in London** – John Ritblat (pc); **There used to be an old tramp** – Shirley Shurville (pc); **army of little grey men** – *Evening Standard*, 23 September 1975; **a larger cigar than usual** – *Observer*, 20 July 1975; **I wouldn't say they're happy** – Cyril Metliss, quoted in *Observer*, 20 July 1975; **Biba was perfectly successful** – *Evening Standard*, 23 September 1975

P.89 **bitten off more** – John Ritblat (pc); **To me the dream was over** – *Evening Standard*, 23 September 1975

P.90 **The big mistake** – quoted in *Independent*, 12 February

1993; **signs mounted on each cash register** – Stanley C Hollander, 'Clio Goes Shopping' in *Arthur Anderson Retailing Issues Letter* Vol 10 Issue 5 (Texas, USA), p.6; **The stock was walking** – John Ritblat (pc); **culpably negligent … theft, etc.** – David Roxburgh, *op. cit.*, 29 October 1974; **The store's pilfering rate** – *Evening Standard*, 23 September 1975; **plain-clothes security** – Yvette Barnett (pc)

P.91 **Biba's time is now unquestionably up** – *Observer*, 20 July 1975; **It was only a minor episode** – John Ritblat (pc); **Sex Pistols gig** – Jon Savage, *England's Dreaming*, p.147; **I knew a girl** – Peter Westcott (pc)

P.92 **Biba Nova** – lyrics by Howard Schuman, music by Andy Mackay; **I'm still sad about it today** – June Russell (pc); **I didn't go in a Dorothy Perkins shop** – Debby Faulkner-Stevens (pc); **I absolutely refused to buy anything** – Anna Ludlow (pc); **I was okay for two days** – *Evening News*, 12 September 1975; **Start another one** – Lewis and Bird *op. cit.*; **It was love at first sight** – *Evening Standard*, 23 September 1975

P.93 **Every time one of our caucus** – *The Times*, 1 April 1976; **debts reckoned to be around £1m** – *Sunday Times*, 9 November 1980; **I liked the tweedy trousers** – *The Times*, 11 November 1980

P.95 **she went on to revamp** – *Globe and Mail* (Toronto, Canada), 27 September 2003; **standard English Terry nappies** – Jan de Villeneuve (pc); **Commerce seems such a bleak** – Genevieve Williams (pc)

INDEX

This book is dedicated to the memory of
Stephen Fitz-Simon and Tim Whitmore

Author's acknowledgements

Primarily I have to thank those people who were kind enough to share their memories of Biba with me: Adam Ant, Andrew Logan, Angie Bowie, Anna Ludlow, Anthea Davies, Antony Little, April Ashley, Barbara Hulanicki, Beth Rayburn, Bob White, Clare Hoffman, Daphne Bewes, Dave Pearce, David Moxey, Debby Faulkner-Stevens, Dizzy Thorne, Elizabeth Imlay, Eleanor Powell, Ellen Haas, Erin Pizzey, George Melly, Genevieve Williams, Ian Dickson, Jan de Villeneuve, John McConnell, John Ritblat, Julie Hodgess, June Russell, Karen Rymer, Kasia Charko, Kate George, Kim Willmott, Lesley Garner, Liz Smith, Malcolm Bird, Marco Pirroni, Michelle Coomber, Mick Rock, Nicky Williams, Norma Kamali, Olivia Temple, Pat Callinan, Peter Westcott, Rosie Young, Sarah Burnett, Sarah E Edgson, Sarah McPherson, Sheila Ruskin, Shirley Shurville, Simon Jenkins, Steve Harley, Steve Thomas, Thamasin Marsh, Toni Franklin, Tony Porter, Trevor Sorbie, Wendy Faehse and Yvette Barnett. This book would have been impossible without their enormous generosity, and I'm deeply grateful to them all. And indeed to the others who didn't want to be named (or who I inadvertently forgot).

I must also thank those who provided further information and contacts: Allison Moore, Bernard O'Neill, Brian Freeborn, Carrie Booth, Chris Angell, Dan Atkinson, Graham Sharpe, John Mindlin, Kate McIntyre, Lisa Wilkinson, Madeline de Vries, Nina Saini, Rik Hull, Robin Headlee, Roger Crimlis, Rosemary Hardin, Sally Waterman, Stella Beddoe, and of course Pari herself. I cannot neglect to mention John Flaxman.

My appreciation too to the staff at the various museums and libraries that I visited: Brighton Museum, British Library, British Newspaper Library, London College of Fashion, Royal College of Art, University of Sussex, Victoria and Albert Museum and Westminster Central Reference Library.

Elizabeth Wilson, Jennifer Lapsley, Lucile Troquet, Peter Westcott, Soren Olsen and Shirley Shurville provided much of the information for the captions to the clothes photographs.'

Mark Eastment is a joy to work with as are, Emily Davies, Juliet Henney, Anna Pearce, Sandy Potkins and Sarah Smye.

Finally, my thanks to Olive Turner, who listened to me wittering on about Biba for months and months.

 Film processing supplied by Primary
www.primary-uk.com

Where possible, approximate dates have been given for the pieces from Pari's collection, but – with tens of thousands of items having been produced by Biba – this is at best an inexact science. Although, therefore, every care has been taken to ensure the accuracy of the descriptions, readers should be aware that exact information has not always been available, and that some pieces may even be dated after the closure of Big Biba in 1975, when the label was reused without Barbara Hulanicki's participation.

Art Direction Isobel Gillan
Editorial Direction Roger Sears

Styling by Pari
Editor Vicki Vrint

©Roger Sears and Isobel Gillan, 2004
World copyright reserved
First published 2004, reprinted, with revisions 2005
Reprinted in 2007
ISBN 978-1-85149-466-8

First published in paperback 2007
ISBN 978-1-85149-541-2

The right of Alwyn Turner to be identified as author of this work has been asserted by him in accordance with the Copyright, Designs and Patents Act 1988

British Library Cataloguing-in-Publication Data

A catalogue record for this book is available from the British Library

Manufactured in China by Imago

Isobel Gillan and Roger Sears wish to thank the following people for their help in preparing this book: Sian Irvine for her beautiful photography and patience throughout and her assistant Byll Pulman for his lighting expertise and good humour; Eileen Driscoll at Don Speake & Co for her help with the mannequins; Sherrie Warwick for hair and make up on all the location photo shoots; the model agencies, who kindly arranged models for the location photo shoots; Francisco at Take Two, Junaidym at Models 1 and Noelle at Storm; the models themselves; Bianca, Hayley, Melody, Jessica, Kathrin and Nina; Dave Farey at HouseStyle Graphics for the use of the Biba typefaces; Steve Thomas for his Biba expertise and the loan of images and artwork, and, finally, Aled Lewis for being more helpful than we had the right to demand.

All photography of the Pari Collection is by Sian Irvine, but we are grateful to the following for the loan of historical illustration: Malcolm Bird 40; Mark Eastment 20; Hulton Getty 10; Neil Libbert 7, 50; Antony Little 21, 36; John McConnell/Pentagram 13, 14, 29, 31, 37, 45, 49; Sarah McPherson 12; Pari Collection 27, 32, 87, 94, 97, 98; Steve Thomas/Whitmore-Thomas 69, 75, 84; Steve Thomas/Whitmore-Thomas /Barbara Hulanicki: 43; Steve Thomas/Whitmore-Thomas/Tim Street-Porter: 9, 65, 67, 74, 81; Steve Thomas/Whitmore-Thomas /Tim White 53, 55, 56, 58, 59, 60, 63, 70, 78, 83, 89, 90, 91; Alwyn W Turner 92; Elizabeth Whiting Associates 35, 41; Kim Willmott 19, 23; Madeleine de Vries 46.